Burn Me A Copy!

Burn Me A Copy!

A compilation of some of the best messages ever sent through the workplace (2000-2005)

Compiled by
Robert D. Kramer

ISBN: 978-0-9895028-2-5

Published in the United States of America

Table of Contents

Introduction

As a background, I am a United States Air Force Vet, and I have spent over 40 years employed in corporate America. Early on in my career, people would come up to me and give me a piece of paper with some sort of joke, story or just an item of interest to read. Usually I got a laugh from it or a comment such as: "That's kool," and "Make me a copy of that." Then after the on-rush of the computers in our business atmosphere, I would get emails from friends and acquaintances of these same type of jokes, stories or items of interest. I would usually laugh, and I almost always printed a copy. Some were dirty in nature, some political, some serious, some short and some had some length to them—you get the picture. I'm sure you have received them too.

I kept most all those copies over the years, and in this book I want to share them with you. I obviously transcribed them onto my computer for the book, but I wrote them just as they were received; spelling, punctuation, language, etc. I think if I put all the copies in a pile, it would probably be 12" to 15" high.

As you read this book, you may see a passage that is duplicated. That means different people sent me that communication in different years. Kind of like, it keeps on giving.

I'm sure as you read these jokes/passages from our past, you may say to yourself, "I remember that." And with others you might say, "That was kool," or "I can relate to that." Either way, I hope you enjoy the book as much as I have enjoyed receiving these jokes, stories and passages over the years.

2000

BOBBY'S YULE LOG

Dear Tim and Cathie:

I've always wanted to do one of these Christmas form letters, but this is the first year our lives have seemed eventful enough to justify doing one. There's so much to share with you, I don't know where to begin. But I couldn't let the holidays pass without wishing you and your family all the very best during this season, and in the next year.

Unfortunately, 2000 began less than auspiciously for me, as I lost my right arm in an IRA car bomb explosion. Luckily for me, however, some local children found it hanging in a tree about thirty yards away, and doctors were able to re-attach it. Regaining control of the arm has been an arduous process, and all the twitches and spasms have caused me some embarrassment. While visiting the London Museum, a spasm in my arm caused me to knock over and smash a 2000 year old Egyptian vase, and only by thinking quickly was I able to blame it on an elderly Norwegian woman who couldn't speak English. I still wonder sometimes what happened to her after the two security guards dragged her away – the look of total bewilderment on her face was priceless. There was another incident, standing close behind a woman on the very crowded train, which I can't go into for legal reasons.

Spring brought better news for the family, as the U.S. Government failed to convict my brother on the Federal Racketeering charges they'd brought against him. Needless to say, he didn't relish the thought of ten years in prison, and he counts himself very fortunate that his attorney, Robert Shapiro, was able to handle things before getting called back to L.A. on some other important case. We all have our fingers crossed that things go equally well next year, when my brother faces the tax-evasion charges. So far, huge legal bills have been the worst part, but they could have been much worse if the mail fraud charges hadn't been dropped for lack of evidence.

1

Jane and I still feel challenged and stimulated by our life together. We've made countless trips to our local grocery store this year, and every time, it seems, we bring home a different combination of goods. Sometimes only one bag, but sometimes up to three or four! To keep things spontaneous, we never decide what we'll buy until we get there. It puts us under pressure, but we think it's a good kind of pressure. We watch television almost continuously, and find it not only entertaining, but even hypnotic sometimes. We even ventured out to a cinema once this year, to see Forest Gump, and we wept at the realization of how nice and simple life would be if only innocence and stupidity could be maintained throughout adulthood. Forrest proved to me that ignorance truly is bliss.

After three years, Jane is still enjoying her job as a ticket-taker at the Tower of London, although the pressure of tearing so many thousands of tickets exactly along the perforation is very stressful sometimes. Tourist love to save the ticket stubs as souvenirs, and some get quite rude if their ticket has a jagged tear. Her boss says she's doing a great job though, and may soon be promoted to selling tickets in the little booth, where she would actually get to handle money and credit cards. Although it's a great job, it's not really what Jane wants to do her entire life. Even after six straight hours of ticket tearing, Jane has made time to attend night school, taking classes to help her get a job at TicketMaster, doing phone sales. It's always been one of Jane's dreams to sit all day at a desk with a phone and a computer on it. Dreams don't always come true, but I have faith in Jane's ability to get what she wants. And after all her hard work she deserves it too – she knows more about tickets than anyone I know.

I'm still unemployed, and it's hard to believe it's been almost two years now! It's amazing how quickly the time flies. If I don't get a job in the nest twelve months, I'll start to have concerns about my prospects. Unless I get some calls, I may have to start reading ads in the paper or going to employment agencies. Several friends have also recommended that I get my resume typed up, instead of using my hand-written one, so I may consider doing that, possibly in the Spring. In the meantime, I continue to earn some spending money by breeding gerbils and selling them outside gay clubs in Soho. It's going so well I may consider franchising my business. Other than that, I'm happy to continue doing as little as possible, and if the blood tests I'm waiting on come back negative, I'll consider myself a lucky man indeed.

Jane and I continue in our efforts to adopt Danny, a 23-year old boy we've grown fond of, but we're still being opposed by Danny's natural parents, who aren't willing to give him up for the $500 we're offering. We'd like to experience parenthood without the trials of infancy or the traumas of teenage years, and the income from his job as a male dancer wouldn't hurt the household budget, either. Since kicking his drug habit he's much less violent, and now that he's engaged to his Iraqi girlfriend, we might even get to be grandparents someday soon. Please keep your fingers crossed for us.

As exciting as our lives are, things can still feel a bit routine sometimes, so last month we decided to splurge and treat ourselves to a holiday. Although it was frivolous, we spent the last of our savings to take advantage of a special offer at the local travel agency – for only $150 each, we got to spend ten days in Sarajevo, right downtown in the Sarajevo Hilton. The travel agent had told us Sarajevo was unspoiled by tourism, and she wasn't kidding – we had the entire 10th floor of the Hilton to ourselves! The agent had warned us that Bosnia was experiencing some sort of political difficulty, but assured us we'd be safe in the hotel if we kept seeing CNN reporters all over the city streets, and they provided me with weather forecasts and sports results. Besides, the hotel manager told us we could stay in any room we wanted to, so when gunfire kept us awake all night, we just moved to quieter rooms. Sightseeing was hard to do, as we constantly had to run from corner to corner, and spent a lot of time cowering and peering around corners. We were usually running too fast to get many good pictures with the camera, so it was no great loss when all our film got confiscated by Serbian soldiers at the airport. It wasn't easy to find a good restaurant either, but we were lucky enough to be there when a shipment of U.N. food supplies arrived in town, so we brought some bottled water and a big sack of rice back to our hotel room. It lasted us almost a week, and saved us some food money as well. All

3

in all it was an exciting vacation, although we could have done without the nuisance of all that sniper fire. Still, like after any trip, it was nice to get back home – I almost forgot how nice it was to use real toilet paper!

And now, here we are, with the Holidays almost upon us again. I can't help getting a little reflective as Christmas approaches, and I'll admit to shedding a few tears when I watch It's A Wonderful Life. I've always felt that people's spirits are higher during the holiday season, and they're nicer to each other. I feel there's just something in the air, besides the normally high levels of carbon monoxide. Maybe people are just happily anticipating the giving and receiving of gifts, the giving and receiving of happiness. But maybe it's something much, much more than that – maybe there's something divine at work here. Maybe. Then again, maybe not, maybe it's just the gifts. Part of it might be all the happy-looking colored lights, but I don't think any of it comes from the fruitcake. Whatever the cause, the spirit of Christmas comes every year about this time, give or take a week, and it never fails to stir in me overwhelming feelings if intense, almost spiritual hunger. I feel compelled, as though by some inner-force, to eat myself into a coma. Sweets and treats everywhere you go, it almost makes Christmas feel like a religious experience to me (if I consume enough chocolate, the sugar buzz can cause me to speak in tongues). And whether or not you find yourself speaking in tongues, we both hope this season is a time of peace, thoughtful meditation, and constant over-eating for you as well.

Please share our sincere good wishes with the entire Johnson family, and we hope you have a beautiful holiday season in Tampa. Even though we haven't spoken to you recently, we still think of you often, and wish you all the best in 2001.

THE ULTIMATE GOLF VACATION

Resourceful Resorts is now offering a fabulous golf vacation to the Middle East.

Trip Includes:
- Round trip airfare on a U.S. Air Force transport aircraft.
- 7 days and 6 nights in Iraq's sole remaining hotel.
- Unlimited admission to Iraq's newly constructed 270,000 hole golf course.
- Featuring:
- A beginner's course with holes up to 30 feet in diameter
- An 83,000 sq. mile sand trap.
- A never ending challenge with new courses being constructed hourly.
- Golf Carts.
- "Hazards" take on a new meaning.
- "Scud" is used in place of "Fore".

Nighttime camel ride for two past romantic Arabian oil fires available at discount rates.

Preferred basement accommodations limited to availability.
From $2,150 DBL Occupancy.

ACCOUNTANTS

What is the definition of an accountant?
Someone who solves a problem you didn't know you had in a way you don't understand.

What's the definition of a good tax accountant?
Someone who has a loophole named after him.

When does a person decide to become an accountant?
When he realizes he doesn't have the charisma to succeed as an undertaker.

What does an accountant use for birth control?
His personality.

What's an extroverted accountant?
One who looks at your shoes while he's talking to you instead of his own.

What's an auditor?
Someone who arrives after the battle and bayonets all the wounded.

Why did the auditor cross the road?
Because he looked in the file and that's what they did last year.

There are three kinds of accountants in the world.
Those who can count and those who can't.

What's an accountant's idea of trashing his hotel room?
Refusing to fill out the guest comment card.

How do you drive an accountant completely insane?
Tie him to a chair, stand in front of him and fold up a road map the wrong way.

What's the most wicked thing a group of young accountants can do?

Go into town and gang-audit someone.

What do accountants suffer from that ordinary people don't?
Depreciation.

An accountant is someone who knows the cost of everything and the value of nothing.

An accountant is having a hard time sleeping and goes to see the doctor. "Doctor, I just can't get to sleep at night."
"Have you tried counting sheep?"
"That's the problem – I make a mistake and then spend three hours trying to find it."

BALLOONIST

A fellow has been learning to be a balloonist and takes his first solo flight. Unfortunately the wind picks up, he is blown off course and is forced to land. He is in a paddock close to a road but has no idea where he is. He sees a car coming along the road and hails it. The driver gets out and the balloonist says. "G'day mate, can you tell me where I am?"

"Yes, of course," says the motorist. "You have just landed in your balloon and with this wind you have obviously been blown off course. You are in the top paddock of John Dawson's farm, 13.5 kilometers from Condobolin. John will be plowing the paddock next week and sowing wheat. There is a bull in the paddock. It is behind you and about to attack you."

At that moment the bull reaches the balloonist and tosses him over the fence. Luckily he is unhurt. He gets up, dusts himself off and says to the motorist, "I see you're an accountant."

"Good Grief," says the other man, "you're right. How did you know that?"

"I employ accountants," says the balloonist. "The information you gave me was detailed, precise and accurate. Most of it was useless and it arrived far too late to be of any help

2001

HMO

Q: What does HMO stand for?
A: This is actually a variation of the phrases, "Hey, Moe!" Its roots go back to a concept pioneered by Dr. Moe Howard of "The Three Stooges" who discovered that a patient could be made to forget about the pain in his foot if he was poked hard enough in the eyes.

Q; I just joined an HMO. How difficult will it be to choose the doctor I want?
A: Just slightly more difficult than choosing your parents. Your insurer will provide you with a book listing all the doctors who were participating in the plan. These doctors basically fall into two categories; those who are no longer accepting new patients, and those who will see you but are no longer part of the plan. But don't worry, the remaining doctors who are still in the plan and accepting new patients has an office just a half-days drive away and that diploma from a small Caribbean Island is very fresh.

Q: Do all diagnostic procedures require pre-certification?
A: No. Only those you need.

Q: What are preexisting conditions?
A: This is a term used by the grammatically challenged when they want to talk about existing conditions. Unfortunately, we appear to be pre-stuck with 'pre and now' meaning the same.

Q: Can I get coverage for my preexisting conditions?
A: Certainly, as long as they don't require any treatment.

Q: What happens if I want to try alternative forms of medicine?
A: You'll need to find alternative forms of payment.

Q: My pharmacy plan only covers generic drugs, but I need the name brand. I tried the generic medication, but it gave me a stomach ache. What should I do?
A: Poke yourself in the eye.

Q: What if I'm away from home and I get sick?
A: You really shouldn't do that.

Q: I think I need to see a specialist, but my doctor insists he can handle my problem. Can a general practitioner really perform a heart transplant right in his office?
A: Hard to say, but considering that all you're risking is the $10 Co-Pay, there is no harm giving him a shot at it.

Q: Will health care be any different in the next century?
A: No. But if you call right now, you might get an appointment by then.

PAUL HARVEY WRITES:

We tried so hard to make things better for out kids that we made them worse. For my grandchildren, I'd like better. I'd really like for them to know about hand me down clothes and homemade ice cream and leftover meat loan sandwiches. I really would.

I hope you learn humility by being humiliated, and that you learn honesty by being cheated. I hope you learn to make your own bed and mow the lawn and wash the car. And I really hope nobody gives you a brand new car when you are sixteen.

It will be good if at least one time you can see puppies born and your old dog put to sleep. I hope you get a black eye fighting for something you believe in. I hope you have to share a bedroom with your younger brother/sister. And it's all right if you have to draw a line down the middle of the room, but when he wants to crawl under the covers with you because he's scared, I hope you let him.

When you want to see a movie and your little brother/sister wants to tags along, I hope you'll let him/her. I hope you have to walk uphill to school with your friends and that you live in a town where you can do it safely. On rainy days when you have to catch a ride, I hope you don't ask your driver to drop you two blocks away so you won't be seen riding with someone as uncool as your Mom.

If you want a slingshot, I hope your Dad teaches you how to make one instead of buying one. I hope you learn to dig in the dirt and read books. When you learn to use computers, I hope you also learn to add and subtract in your head.

I hope you get teased by your friends when you have your first crush on a boy/girl, and when you talk back to your mother that you learn what ivory soap tastes like. May you skin your knee climbing a mountain, burn your hand on a stove and stick you tongue on a frozen flagpole.

I don't care if you try a beer once, but I hope you don't like it. And if a friend offers you dope or a joint, I hope you realize he is not your friend. I sure hope you make time to sit on a porch with your Grandpa/Grandma and go fishing with your Uncle.

11

May you feel sorrow at a funeral and joy during the holidays. I hope your mother punishes you when you throw a baseball through your neighbor's window and that she hugs you and kisses you at Hanukah/Christmas time when you give her a plaster mold of your hand.

These things I wish for you – tough times and disappointment, hard work and happiness. To me, it's the only way to appreciate life. Written with a pen. Sealed with a kiss. I'm here for you. And if I die before you do, I'll go to heaven and wait for you.

Send this to all of your friends. We secured our friends, not by accepting favors, but by doing them

2002

EXPRESSIONS FOR WOMEN ON HIGH STRESS DAYS

1. You - Off my planet.
2. Not the brightest crayon in the box now are we?
3. Well, this day was a total waste of makeup.
4. Errors have been made. Others will be blamed.
5. And your crybaby whiny-assed opinion would be …?
6. I'm not crazy, I've just been in a very bad mood for 30 years.
7. Allow me to introduce my selves.
8. Sarcasm is just one more service we offer.
9. Whatever kind of look you were going for, you missed.
10. I'm just working here until a good fast-food job opens up.
11. I'm trying to imagine you with a personality.
12. Stress is when you wake up screaming and you realize you weren't asleep.
13. I can't remember if I'm the good twin or the evil one.
14. How many times do I have to flush before you go away?
15. I just want revenge. Is that so wrong?
16. You say I'm a bitch like that's a bad thing.
17. Can I trade this job for what's behind door #2?
18. Nice perfume. Must you marinate in it?
19. Chaos, panic, and disorder - my work here is done.
20. Earth is full. Go home.
21. Is it time for your medication or mine?
22. How do I set a laser printer to stun?
23. I'm not tense, just terribly, terribly alert.

MARRIAGE SECRETS

My wife and I have the secret to making our marriage last:

1. Two times a week, we go to a nice restaurant, have a little wine, some good food and companionship. She goes on Tuesdays, I go on Friday's.

2. We also sleep in separate beds. Hers is in Florida and mine in Cincinnati.

3. I take my wife everywhere, but she keeps finding her way back.

4. I asked my wife where she wanted to go for our anniversary. "Somewhere I haven't been in a long time!" she said. So, I suggested the kitchen.

5. We always hold hands. If I let go, she shops.

6. She has an electric blender, electric toaster, and electric bread maker. Then she said, "There are too many gadgets, and no place to sit down!" So I bought her an electric chair.

7. She ran after the garbage truck, yelling, "Am I too late for the garbage?" The driver said, "No jump in!"

8. Remember .... Marriage is the number one cause of divorce. Statistically, 100% of all divorces started with marriage.

9. The last fight was my fault. My wife asked, "What's on the TV?" I said, "Dust."

HUSBAND REFLECTS ON 20 YEARS OF MARRIAGE

A woman awakes during the night to find her husband was not in bed. She puts on her robe and goes downstairs to look for him. She finds him sitting at the kitchen table with a cup of coffee in front of him. He appears to be in deep thought, just staring at the wall. She watches as he wiped a tear from his eye and takes a sip of his coffee. "What's the matter, dear?" She whispers as she steps into the room, "why are you down here at this time of night?"

The husband looks up from his coffee, "Do you remember 20 years ago when we were dating, and you were only 16?" He asks solemnly.

"Yes I do", she replies. The husband paused. The words were not coming easily. "Do you remember when your father caught us in the back seat of my car making love?"

Yes, I remember" said the wife, lowering herself into a chair besides him. The husband continued … "Do you remember when he shoved the shotgun in my face and said, "Either you marry my daughter, or I'll send you to jail for 20 years?"

"I remember that too" she replied softly. He wiped another tear from his cheek and said. "I would have gotten out today."

DISORDER IN THE COURT

Statements people actually said in court, word for word, taken down and now published by court reporters.

Judge: "Well, Sir, I have reviewed this case and I've decided to give your wife 4775 a week."
Husband: "That's fair, your honor. I'll try to send her a few bucks myself."

Q: What is your date of birth?
A: July fifteenth.
Q: What year?
A: Every year.

Q: What gear were you in at moment of the impact?
A: Gucci sweats and Reeboks.

Q: This myasthenia gravis, does it affect your memory at all?
A: Yes.
Q: And in what ways does it affect your memory?
A: I forget.
Q: You forget. Can you give us an example of something you've forgotten?

Q: How old is your son, the one living with you.
A: Thirty-eight or thirty-five, I can't remember which.
Q: How long has he lived with you?
A: Forty-five years.

Q: What was the first thing your husband said to you when he woke up that morning?
A: He said, "Where am I, Cathy?"
Q: And why did that upset you?
A: My name is Susan.

Q: And where was the location of the accident?

A: Approximately milepost 499.
Q: And where is milepost 499?
A: Probably between milepost 498 and 500.

Q: Sir, what is your IQ?
A: Well I can see pretty well, I think.

Q: Did you blow your horn or anything?
A: After the accident?
Q: Before the accident.
A: Sure, I played for 10 years. I even went to school for it.

Q: Trooper, when you stopped the defendant, were your red and blue lights flashing?
A: Yes
Q: Did the defendant say anything when she got out of her car?
A: Yes, sir.
Q: What did she say?
A: What disco am I at?

Q: Now doctor, isn't it true that when a person dies in his sleep, he doesn't know about it until the next morning?

Q: The youngest son, the 20-year old, how old is he?

Q: Were you present when your picture was taken?

Q: So the date of conception of (the baby) was August 8th?
A: Yes.
Q: And what were you doing at that time?

Q: She had three children, right?
A: Yes.
Q How many were boys?
A: None.
Q: Were there any girls?

Q: You say the stairs went down to the basement?

A: Yes.
Q: And these stairs, did they go up also?

Q: How was your first marriage terminated?
A: By death.
Q: And by whose death was it terminated?

Q: Can you describe the individual?
A: He was about medium height and had a beard.
Q: Was this a male or a female?

Q: Is your appearance here this morning pursuant to a deposition that I sent to your attorney?
A: No, this is how I dress when I go to work.

Q: Doctor, how many autopsies have you performed on dead people?
A: All my autopsies are performed on dead people.

Q: All your responses must be oral, OK?
A: OK.
Q: What school did you go to?
A: Oral

Q: Do you recall the time that you examined the body?
A: The autopsy started around 8:30 p.m.
Q: And Mr. Dennington was dead at the time?
A: No, he was sitting on the table wondering why I was doing an autopsy.

Q: Are you qualified to give a urine sample?

Q: Doctor, before you performed the autopsy, did you check for a pulse?
A: No.
Q: Did you check for blood pressure?
A: No.
Q: Did you check for breathing?
A: No.

Q: So, then it is possible that the patient was alive when you began the autopsy?

A: No.

Q: How can you be so sure, Doctor?

A: Because his brain was sitting on my desk in a jar.

Q: But could the patient have still been alive nevertheless?

A: Yes, it is possible that he could have been alive and practicing law somewhere.

ALLIGATORS

Two alligators are sitting on the edge of a swamp. The small one turns to the big one and says; I don't understand how you can be so much bigger than me. We're the same age, we were the same size as kids …. I just don't get it.

"Well." Says the big alligator, "What have you been eating?"
"Lawyers, same as you," replies the small alligator.
"Hm. Well, where do you catch'em?"
"Down at the law firm on the edge of the swamp."
"Same here. Hm. How do you catch'em?"

"Well, I crawl under a BMW and wait for someone to unlock the door. Then I jump out, bite'em , shake the shit out of 'em, and eat'em!"

"Ah!" says the big alligator, "I think I see your problem. See, by the time you get done shaken' the shit out of a lawyer, there's nothing left but lips and a briefcase …"

NO EXCUSE SUNDAYS

In order to make it possible for everyone to attend church next week we are planning a special No Excuse Sunday ....

1. Cots will be placed in vestibules for those who say, "Sunday is my only day for sleeping in."

2. Eye drops will be available for those whose eyes are tired from watching TV too late on Saturday night.

3. We will have steel helmets for those who believe the roof will cave in if they show up for church services.

4. Blankets will be furnished for those who complain that the church is too cold. Fans will be on hand for those who say the church is too hot.

5. We will have hearing aids for the parishioners who say, "The pastor doesn't talk loud enough." There will be cotton balls for those who say, "The pastor talks too loud."

6. Score cards will be available for those who wish to count the hypocrites.

7. We guarantee that some relatives will be present for those who like to go visiting on Sunday.

8. There will be TV dinners available for those who claim they can't go to church and cook dinner too.

9. One section of the church will have some trees and grass for those who see God in nature ... especially on the golf course.

10. The sanctuary will be decorated with both Christmas poinsettias and Easter lilies to create a familiar environment for those who have never seen the church without them.

See You Sunday!!

NEW INVESTMENTS

In the wake of the Exxon/Mobil deal and the AOL/Time Warner implode, I want to make a few close friends aware of the next expected mergers so you can get in on the ground floor and make some BIG Bucks.

- Hale Business Systems, Mary Kay Cosmetics, Fuller Brush and W.R.Grace will merge and become Hale, Mary, Fuller, Grace.

- Polygram Records, Warner Bros. and Zesta Crackers join forces and become ... Polly, Warner Cracker.

- 3M will merge with Goodyear and issue forth as MMMGood.

- Zippo Mfg., Audi, Motor Car, Dofasco and Dakota Mining will merge to become, of course, Zip AudiDoDa.

- Federal Express is expected to join its major competitor, UPS, and consolidate as FedUp.

- Fairchild Electronics and Honeywell Computers will become Fairwell Honeychild.

- Gray Poupon and Docker Pants are expected to become Poupon Pants.

- Knotts Berry Farm and the Nat'l Org. of Women will become Knott NOW!

HUGE BLACK GUY

A skinny white guy goes into an elevator, looks up and sees this HUGE black guy standing next to him. The big guy sees the little guy staring at him, looks down and says, "7 feet tall, 350 pounds, 20 inch penis, 3 pound left testicle and 3 pound right testicle, Turner Brown."

The small guy faints dead away and falls to the floor. The big dude kneels down and brings him to, slapping his face and shaking him. When the little guy finally comes around, the big guy asks him, "What's wrong with you?"

In a very weak voice the little guy says, "Excuse me, but what EXACTLY did you say to me?"

The big dude said, "I saw the curious look on your face and figured I'd just give you the answers to the questions everyone always asks me. I'm 7 feet tall, I weigh 350 pounds, I have a 20 inch penis, my left testicle weighs 3 pounds, my right testicle weighs 3 pounds and my name is Turner Brown."

The small guy says, "Thank God! I thought you said, 'Turn around.'"

A REAL PROBLEM

Be sure to cancel your credit cards before you die ...

My Aunt died this past January. Citi Bank billed her for February and March for their monthly service charge on her credit card, and then added late fees and interest on the monthly charge ... the balance had been $0.00 ... now was somewhere around $60.00.

I placed the following phone call to CitiBank:
Me: "I am calling to tell you that my aunt died in January."

CitiBank: "The account was never closed and the late fees and charges still apply."

Me: "Maybe you should turn it over to collections ..."

CitiBank: "Since it is 2 months past due, it already has been."

Me: "So, what will they do when they find out she is dead?"

CitiBank: "Either report her account to the frauds division, or report her to the credit bureau ... maybe both."

Me: "Do you think God will be mad at her?"

CitiBank: " ... excuse me.?"

Me: "Did you just get what I was telling you ... the past about her being dead?"

CitiBank: "Sir, you'll have to speak to my supervisor!"
         (Supervisor gets on the phone)

Me: "I'm calling to tell you, my aunt died in January."

CitiBank: "The account was never closed and the late fees and charges still apply."

Me: "You mean you want to collect from her estate?"

CitiBank: "... (stammer)". "Are you her lawyer?"

Me: "No, I'm her great nephew." (Lawyer info given ...)

CitiBank: "Could you fax us a certificate of death?"

Me: "Sure." (Fax number is given)
          (after they get the fax)

CitiBank: "Our system just isn't set up for death ..."

Me: "Oh."

CitiBank: "I don't know what more I can do to help ..."

Me: Well ... if you figure it out, great! If not, you could just keep billing her ... I suppose ... don't really think she will care ..."

CitiBank: "Well ... the late fees and charges do still apply."

Me: "Would you like her new billing address?"

CitiBank: "That might help."

Me: Odessa Memorial Cemetery, Highway 129, and plot number given with city, state and zip code.

CitiBank: "Sir, that's a cemetery!"

Me: "What do you do with dead people on your planet?!!"

OHIO FACTS AND TRIVIA

1. The first ambulance service was established in Cincinnati in 1865.

2. Cleveland boasts America's first traffic light. It began on August 5, 1914.

3. Ermal Franz invented the pop-top can in Kettering.

4. James J. Ritty, of Dayton, invented the cash register in 1879 to stop his patrons from pilfering house profits.

5. "Hang On Sloopy" is the official state rock song.

6. Cincinnati reds were the first professional baseball team.

7. The Y Bridge in Zanesville was first built in 1814 to span the confluence of the licking and Muskingum Rivers. The current bridge is the fifth construction at the same location. "Ripley's Believe It or Not" proclaimed it the only bridge in the world which you can cross and still be on the same side of the river.

8. Akron was the first city to use police cars.

9. Cincinnati had the first professional city fire department.

10. Akron is the rubber capital of the world.

11. The American Federation of Labor was founder in Columbus.

12. Ohio Senator John Glenn became the oldest man to venture into outer space. On February 20, 1962 he was the first American to orbit the earth. In October of 1998 at the age of 77 he returned to the space program and traveled back into space.

13. Cleveland is home to the Rock and Roll Hall of Fame.

14. Ohio is the leading producer of greenhouse and nursery plants.

15. The Pro Football Hall of Fame is located in Canton.

16. Neil Armstrong became the first man to walk on the moon. He was from Wapakoneta.

17. The Wright Brothers are acknowledged as inventors of the first airplane. They were from Dayton.

18. East Liverpool was the beginning point of the United States Public Land Survey. The location was the area from which a rectangular-grid land survey system was established under the Ordinance of 1785. The survey provided for administration and subdivision of land in the Old Northwest Territory. The Ordinance stipulated that all public lands were to be divided into townships six miles square.

19. Seven United States presidents were born in Ohio. They are: Ulysses S. Grant, Rutherford B. Hayes, James A. Garfield, Benjamin Harrison, William McKinley, William H. Taft, and Warren G. Harding.

FIFTY YEARS AGO

An elderly couple is enjoying an anniversary dinner together in a small tavern. The husband leans over and asks his wife, "Do you remember the first time we had sex together over fifty years ago? We went behind this tavern where you leaned against the fence and I made love to you." "Yes," she says, "I remember it well." "OK," he says, "how about taking a stroll round there again and we can do it for old time's sake?"

"Ooooooh Henry, you devil, that sounds like a good idea," she answers.

There's a police officer sitting in the next booth listening to all this, and having a chuckle to himself. He thinks, "I've got to see these tow old-timers having sex against a fence. I'll just keep an eye on them so there's no trouble." So he follows them. They walk haltingly along, leaning on each other for support, aided my walking sticks.

Finally they get to the back of the tavern and make their way to the fence. The old lady lifts her skirt, takes her knickers down and the old man drops his trousers. She turns around and as she hangs on to the fence, the old man moves in. Suddenly they erupt into the most furious sex that the watching policeman has ever seen

They are bucking and jumping like eighteen-year-olds. This goes on for about forty minutes! She's yelling, "Ohhh, God!" He's hanging on to her hips for dear life. This is the most athletic sex imaginable. Finally, they both collapse panting on the ground.

The policeman is amazed. He thinks he has learned something about life that he didn't know. After about half an hour of lying on the ground recovering, the old couple struggle to their feet and put their clothes back on. The policeman, still watching thinks, that was truly amazing, he was going like a train. I've got to ask him what his secret is. As the couple passes, he says to them, "That was something else! You must have been having sex for about forty minutes. How do you manage it? You must have had a fantastic life together. Is there some sort of secret?"

The old man says, "Fifty years ago that wasn't an electric fence."

2003

BUCS FAN

A first grade teacher in Philadelphia explains to her class that she is an Eagle fan. She asks her students to raise their hands if they too are Eagle fans. Everyone in the class raises their hand, except one little girl. The teacher looks at the little girl with surprise and says, "Janie, why didn't you raise your hand?"

"Because I'm not an Eagle fan," she replied.

The teacher, still shocked, asked, "Well, if you are not an Eagles fan, then who are you a fan of?"

"I'm a Buccaneers fan, and proud of it," Janie replied. The teacher could not believe her ears. "Janie, why are you a Buccaneer fan?"

"Because my mom is a Buccaneers fan, and my dad is a Buccaneers fan, so I'm a Buccaneers fan too."

"Well," said the teacher in an obviously annoyed tone, "that is no reason for you to be a Buccaneers fan. You don't have to be just like your parents all of the time. What if your mom was a moron and your dad was a moron, what would you be then?"

"Then," Janie smiled, "we'd be Eagles fans."

HE WHO SINS

Bill Clinton, Al Gore and George W. Bush died and found themselves standing on the other side of the Jordan River, looking across at the Promised Land.

The Archangel Michael was standing on the other side and shouted over to the three surprised Americans, "Contrary to what you have been taught, each of you will have to wade across the Jordan River."

As Michael saw their perplexed looks, he reassured them by saying, "Don't worry. You will sink only proportionally according to your sins on earth. The more you have sinned the more you will sink into the water."

The three American sages of political lore looked at one another, trying to determine who shall be the first brave soul to cross the Jordan.

Finally George W. Bush volunteered to go first. Slowly he began to wade out into the river, and slowly the water began to get higher and higher, reaching his waist. George began to sweat, thinking that all of his sins were coming back to haunt him. He was beginning to wonder if he would ever see the other side. Finally, after what seemed like an eternity, he began to emerge on the river's bank. As he ascended to the other side, he looked behind him to see which one of the other brave souls was going next. A shock of surprise registered on his face, as he saw Al Gore almost in the middle of the river and only his ankles barely touching the water.

He turned to Michael and exclaimed, "I know Al Gore was a friend of mine, and he has sinned much, much more than that."

Archangel Michael replied, "He's standing on Clinton's shoulders!"

TWAS A WEEK AFTER CHRISTMAS

T'was a week after Christmas and all through the stands,
Everybody was cheering, and clapping their hands.
The talk had been spirited, setting the stage …
A postseason battle was not set to wage.

The Buckeyes were underdogs (based on the spread).
But visions of victory danced in their heads.
And Ma in her jersey and I in my cap,
Were set on the sofa to watch the first snap.

When there on the TV arose such a fuss,
I inched myself forward and tried not us cuss.
I rose to my feet and I stomped on the ground,
I grabbed the remote and turned off the sound.

The sight wasn't pretty, my Bucks were behind,
(What's worse, they were playing a team I maligned).
Then what on the flickering screen did I see,
But a great Buckeye offense and some awesome D.

The QB was quick with an arm like a cannon,
I knew in a moment it wasn't Belasari.
With Vick-like scrambles and Montana-like aim,
He guided his offense and called them by name.

"To Jenkins, to Gamble, to Hartsock and to Vance,
Run Ross, run Hall, run Clarett, first down'
Hammer the middle and throw the long ball,
Now down the field, down the field, down the field all.

When e'er he felt pressure he scrambled away,
And gave up not one single sack the whole day.
He passed on the defense with quickness and speed
(The way teachers in Ann Arbor pass kids who can't read).

32

Like high powered bullets through a paper fence,
We tore through that defense, like Buckeyes possessed.
Tackles were broken and coverages blown,
And next thing I knew, we were in the end zone.

After winning the game for the scarlet and gray,
Craig ran for the showers without looking away.
But I heard him exclaim as he grinned in delight, "Merry Christmas
Miami, we turned out your lights."

COMPUTERS AND CARS

For all of us who feel only the deepest love and affection for the way computers have enhanced our lives, read on.

At a recent computer expo (COMDEX), Bill Gates reportedly compared the computer industry with the auto industry and stated, "If GM had kept up with the technology like the computer industry has, we would all be driving $25.00 cars that gets 1,000 miles to the gallon."

The response to Bill's comments, General Motors issued a press release stating: If GM had developed technology like Microsoft, we would all be driving cars with the following characteristics:

1. For no reason whatsoever, your car would crash twice a day.
2. Every time they repainted the lines in the road, you would have to buy a new car.
3. Occasionally your car would die on the freeway for no reason. You would have to pull over to the side of the road, close all of the windows, shut off the car, restart it, and reopen the windows before you could continue. For some reason you would simply accept this.
4. Occasionally, executing a maneuver such as a left turn would cause your car to shut down and refuse to restart, in which case you would have to reinstall the engine.
5. Macintosh would make a car that was powered by the sun, was reliable, five times as fast and twice as easy to drive – but would run only five percent of the roads.
6. The oil, water temperature, and alternator warning lights would all be replaced by a single "This Car Has Performed an Illegal Operation" warning light.
7. The airbag system would ask "Are you sure?" before deploying.

8. Occasionally, for no reason whatsoever, your car would lock you out and refuse to let you in until you simultaneously lifted the door handle turned the key and grabbed hold of the radio antenna.

9. Every time a new car was introduced, car buyers would have to learn how to drive all over again, because none of the controls would operate in the same manner as the old car.

10. You'd have to press the "Start" button to turn the engine off.

RECEIVED JUST AFTER THE BUCCANEERS WON THE SUPER BOWL

Troy Aikman, after living a full life, died. When he got to heaven, God was showing him around. They came to a modest little house with a faded Cowboys flag in the window. "This house is yours for eternity, Troy," said God. "This is very special; not everyone gets a house up here."

Troy felt special, indeed, and walked up to his house. On his way up the porch, he noticed another house just around the corner. It was a huge 3-story mansion with a Red and Pewter sidewalk, a 50-foot tall flagpole with an enormous Bucs flag, and Bucs pennants hung in every window. Troy looked at God and said, "God, I'm not trying to be ungrateful, but I have a question. I was an all-pro QB, and I won Super Bowls."

God said, "So what do you want to know, Troy?"

"Well, why will Brad Johnson get a better house than me?"

God chuckled, and said, "Troy, that's not Brad Johnson' house, it's mine. Go Bucs!!"

YOU KNOW YOU ARE
LIVING IN THE YEAR 2003 WHEN:

- Your reason for not staying in touch with family is because they do not have e-mail.

- You have a list of 15 phone numbers to reach your family of three.

- Your grandmother asks you to send her a JPEG file of your newborn so she can create a screen saver.

- You pull up in your own driveway and use your cell phone to see if anyone is home.

- Every commercial on television has a web site address at the bottom of the screen.

- You buy a computer and 3 months later it's out of date and sells for half the price you paid.

- Leaving the house without your cell phone, which you didn't have the first 20 or 30 (or 60) years of your life, is now a cause for panic and you turn around to go get it.

- Using real money, instead of credit or debit, to make a purchase would be a hassle and take planning.

- You just tried to enter your password on the microwave.

- You consider second-day air delivery painfully slow.

- Your dining room table is now your flat filing cabinet.

- Your idea of being organized is multiple colored Post-it notes.

- You hear most of your jokes via e-mail instead of in person.

- You get an extra phone line so you can get phone calls.

- You disconnect from the Internet and get this awful feeling, as if you just pulled the plug on a loved one.

- You get up in the morning and go on line before getting your coffee.

- You wake up at 2 AM to go to the bathroom and check your e-mail on your way back to bed.

- You start tilting your head sideways to smile. :)

- You're reading this and nodding and laughing.

- Even worse; you know exactly who you are going to forward this to....

STAR TREK

The Iraqi Ambassador to the UN has just finished giving a speech, and walks out into the lobby where he meets President Bush.

They shake hands and as they walk the Iraqi says, "You know, I have just one question about what I have seen in America."

President Bush says, "Well, Mr. Ambassador, anything I can do to help you, I will do."

The Iraqi whispers, "My son watches this show 'Star Trek' and in it there are Russians and Blacks and Whites and Asians and Jews, but never any Arabs. He is very upset. He doesn't understand why there are never any Arabs in 'Star Trek.'"

President Bush chuckles and leans toward the Iraqi, and whispers back, "It's because it takes place in the future."

CRUSHED NUTS

A little old man shuffled slowly into an ice cream parlor, crawled painfully onto a stool, and ordered a banana split.

The waitress asked, "Crushed nuts?"

"No," he replies, "It's just arthritis."

OHIO STORMS

Dear Diary:

Aug. 12 - Moved to Ohio. It is so beautiful here. The rolling green hills are so nice. Can hardly wait to see snow covering them.

Oct. 14 - Ohio is the most beautiful place on earth. The leaves are turned all the colors and shades of red and orange. Went for a ride through the beautiful hills and saw some deer. They are so graceful. Certainly they are the most wonderful animal on earth. This must be paradise, I love it here.

Nov. 11 - Deer season will start soon. I can't imagine anyone wanting to kill such a gorgeous creature. Hope it will start to snow soon. I love it here.

Dec. 2 - It snowed last night. Woke up to find everything blanketed in white. It looks like a postcard. We went outside and cleaned the snow off the steps and shoveled the driveway. We had a snowball fight (I won), and when the snowplow came by, we had to shovel the driveway again.

Dec 19 - More snow last night. Couldn't get out of the driveway to get to work. I am exhausted from shoveling the driveway. Butthole!

Dec. 25 - Merry Frickin Christmas. More frikken snow. If I ever get my hands on that son-of-a-b**ch who drives the snowplow I swear I'll kill the ba$*rd. Don't know why they don't use more salt on the roads to melt the %$#& ice.

Dec. 27 - More white crap last night. Been inside for three days except for shoveling out the driveway after that snowplow goes through every time. Can't go anywhere, cars stuck in a mountain of white crap. The weatherman says to expect another 10" of the crap again tonight. Do you know how many shovels full of snow 10" is?

Dec 28 - The fricking weatherman was wrong. We got 34" of that white crap this time. At this rate it won't melt before summer. The snowplow got stuck up in the road and that ba$*ard came to the door and asked to borrow my shovel. And I told him I had broken six shovels already shoveling all the crap he pushed into the driveway, I broke my last one over his %$#& head.

Jan. 4 - Finally got out of the house today. Went to the store to get food and on the way back a @%#&^ deer ran in front of my car and I hit it. Did about $3000 damage to the car. Those %$#&^ beasts should be killed. Wish the hunters had killed them all last November.

May 3 - Took the car to the garage in town. Would you believe the thing is rusting out from the fricking salt they put all over the roads?

May 10 - Moved to Florida. I can't imagine why anyone in their right mind would ever live in that God-forsaken State of Ohio.

THREE GRANDMAS

Three ornery grandmas were sitting on a bench outside a nursing home. An elderly man walked by and one of the grandmas said, "We bet we can tell how old you are." The old man said, "There ain't no way you can guess it." One of the ornery grandmas said, "Sure we can! Drop your pants."

He did. The old grandmas stared at him for a while. Then they all piped up and said in unison, "You're 84 years old!"

The old man was stunned. "Amazing. How did you guess that?" The ornery old grandmas began laughing and slapping their knees and said, "You told us yesterday."

HOW TO SAY "I LOVE YOU" IN 17 LANGUAGES

English	I Love You
Spanish	Re Amo
French	Je T'aime
German	Ich Liebe Dich
Italian	Ti Amo
Chinese	Wo Ai Ni
Swedish	Jag Alskar

Alabama, Arkansas, Georgia, Tennessee, Missouri, Mississippi, Montana, Louisiana, Virginia, West Virginia, and Kentucky.... Nice Ass, Get in the truck!

WILL HE JUMP

A redhead walked into a sports bar around 9:58 PM. She sat down next to a blonde at the bar and stares up at the TV. The 10:00 news was on. The news crew was covering a story of a man on a ledge of a large building preparing to jump. The redhead turned to the blonde and says. "You know, I bet he'll jump." The blonde replied, "Well, I bet he won't."

The redhead placed $20 on the bar, the guy did a swan dive off of the building, falling to his death. The blonde was very upset and handed her $20 dollars to the redhead and said, "All is fair. Here is your money."

The redhead replied, "Honey, I can't take your money, I saw this earlier on the early news."

"I know," said the blonde, "I saw it on the 5 o'clock news too, but I didn't think he would do it again."

AIRPLANE DOWN

An airplane was going down & everybody knew they would crash in the ocean below. A rich lady takes off all of her clothes and puts on every diamond she has on her body!

The passengers all look at her and say what are you doing? She says, "When we are in the ocean my diamonds will sparkle and I will be the first one they find."

Then another woman takes off all her clothes and covers herself with $100 dollar bills. The passengers all look at her, and she says, "When we are in the ocean the $100 dollar bills will be floating all around me and they will find me first?"

The black lady tears off all her clothes and just gets butt-naked!!

All passengers look at her and ask, "What are you doing?" The black lady says … "GIRL!!!, you know they always look for the black box first!!"

OUT YOU GO

The train was very crowded, so the soldier walked the length of the train, looking for an empty seat. The only unoccupied seat was directly adjacent to a well-dressed middle-aged French lady and was being used by her little dog. The war-weary soldier asked, "Please ma'am, may I sit in that seat?"

The French woman looked down her nose at the soldier, sniffed and said, "You Americans. You are such a rude class of people, Can't you see my Little Fifi is using that seat?"

The soldier walked away, determined to find a place to rest, but after another trip down to the end of the train, found himself again facing the woman with the dog. Again he asked, "Please, lady. May I sit there? I'm very tired."

The French woman wrinkled her nose and snorted, "You Americans! Not only are you rude, you are also arrogant."

Imagine! The soldier didn't say anything else; he leaned over, picked up the little dog, tossed it out the window of the train and sat down in the empty seat. The woman shrieked and railed, and demanded that someone defend her and chastise the soldier.

An English gentleman sitting across the aisle spoke up. "You know, sir, you Americans do seem to have a penchant for doing the wrong thing. You eat holding the fork in the wrong hand. You drive your autos on the wrong side of the road. And now, sir, you've thrown the wrong bitch out the window."

DATING IN 1957

It's the Spring of 1957 and Bobby goes to pick up his date, Peggy Sue. Bobby's a pretty hip guy with his own car and a ducktail hairdo. When he goes to the front door, Peggy Sue's father answers and invites him in.

"Peggy Sue's not ready yet, so why don't you have a seat," he says. "That's cool" says Bobby. Peggy Sue's father asks Bobby what they are planning to do. Bobby replies politely that they will probably just go to the malt shop or to a drive-in movie. Peggy Sue's father responds, "Why don't you kids go out and screw? I hear all the kids are doing it."

Naturally this comes as quite a surprise to Bobby and he says, "Whaaaaat?"

"Yeah," says Peggy Sue's father, "Peggy Sue really likes to screw. She'll screw all night if we let her." Bobby eyes light up and he smiles from ear to ear. Immediately, he has revised the plans for the evening.

A few minutes later, Peggy Sue comes downstairs in her little poodle skirt with her saddle shoes and announces that she's ready to go.

Almost breathless with anticipation, Bobby escorts his date out the front door while dad is saying "Have a good evening kids," with a wink.

About 20 minutes later, a thoroughly disheveled Peggy Sue rushes back into the house, slams the door behind her and screams at her father: "DAMMIT DADDY! THE TWIST!!!! IT'S CALLED THE TWIST!!!!"

THE TOP TEN

Top 10 messages left on Mike Weir's answering machine after he won the Masters.

1. "Congratulations and, oh yeah, who the hell are you?"
2. "This is the Canadian Gold Hall of Fame. Want to be our first member?"
3. "It's Tiger Woods. Finishing 15th would feel much worse if it weren't for my 62 million dollars in endorsements."
4. "Dude, I was so drunk when I was watching the Masters, I actually thought you won."
5. "It's Tiger again. Seriously, give me the damn jacket."
6. "This is President Bush. Today you made all of us proud to be Canadian."
7. "Crap, must've misdialed. I was trying to reach Jose Maria Olazabal."
8. "Hootie Johnson here. Victory dinner is on me, but don't bring your wife."
9. "I see you've used some of your prize money to buy an answering machine."
10. "You seem to be good at sports – can you play for the Mets?"

WHY MUSLIM TERRORISTS
ARE SO QUICK TO COMMIT SUICIDE

Everyone seems to be wondering why Muslim terrorists are so quick to commit suicide.

Let's see now ……..

No beer.
No booze.
No bars.
No television.
No cheerleaders.
No NASCAR.
No NHRA.
No baseball.
No Football.
No hockey.
No golf.
No tailgate parties.
No Hooters.
No pork BBQ.
No hot dogs.
No burgers.
No outboard motors.
No lobster, shellfish, or even Mrs. Paul's frozen fish sticks.
Rags for clothes and towels for hats.
Constant wailing from the guy in the tower.
No chocolate chip cookies.
No Victoria's Secret catalogs.
No super bowl parties.
No Christmas.
You can't shave.
Your wife can't shave.
You can't shower to wash off the smell of donkey cooked over burning camel dung.
The women have to wear baggy dresses and veils at all times.

Your bride is picked by someone else.

She smells just like your donkey, but your donkey has a better disposition.

Then they tell you that when you die it all gets better!

No mystery here!

VIAGRA

Pfizer Corp. is making the announcement today that VIAGRA will soon be available in liquid form, and will be marketed by Pepsi Cola as a power beverage suitable for use as a mixer. It will now be possible for a man to literally pour himself a stiff one.

Obviously, we can no longer call this a soft drink, ad it gives new meaning to the terms "cocktails", and plain old "stiff drink". Pepsi will market the new concoction by the name of ….. "Mount And Do".

A POEM FOR COMPUTER USERS OVER 40

A computer was something on TV
From a Science Fiction show of note
A Window was something you hated to clean
And Ram was the father of a goat.

Meg was the name of my girlfriend
And Gig was a job for the nights
Now they all mean different things
And that really Mega Bytes.

An Application was for employment
A Program was a TV show
A Cursor used profanity
A keyboard was a piano.

A Memory was something that you lost with age
A CD was a bank account
And if you had a 3-inch floppy
You hoped nobody found out.

Compress! It was something you did to the garbage
Not something you did to a file
And if you unzipped anything in public
You'd be in jail for a while.

Log on was adding wood to the fire
Hard drive was a long trip on the road
A Mouse Pad was where a mouse lived
And a Backup happened to your commode.

Cut you did with a pocket knife
Paste you did with glue
A Web was a spider's home
And a Virus was the flu.

I guess I'll stick to my pad and paper
And the Memory in my head.
I hear nobody's been killed in a Computer Crash
But when it happens they wish they were dead.

STATE MOTTOS

Alabama: Hell yes, we have electricity.

Alaska: 11,623 Eskimos can't be wrong.

Arizona: But it's dry heat.

Arkansas: Literacy ain't everything.

California: By 30, our women have more plastic than your Honda.

Colorado: If you don't ski, don't bother.

Connecticut: Like Massachusetts, only the Kennedy's don't own it yet.

Delaware: We really do like the chemicals in out water.

Florida: Ask us about our grandkids.

Georgia: We put the "fun" in fundamentalist extremism.

Hawaii: Haka Tiki Mou DSha'ami Leeke Toru (Death to mainland scum. Leave your money.

Idaho: More than just potatoes … well okay, we're not, but the potatoes are real good.

Illinois: Please don't pronounce the "S".

Indiana: 2 billion years tidal wave free.

Iowa: We do amazing things with corn.

Kansas: First of the rectangle states.

Kentucky: Five million people; fifteen last Names.

Louisiana: We're not all drunken Cajun wackos, but that's our tourism campaign.

Maine: We're really cold, but we have cheap Lobster.

Maryland: If you can dream it, we can tax it.

Massachusetts: Our taxes are lower than Sweden's (for most tax brackets).

Michigan: First line of defense from the Canadians.

Minnesota: 10,000 lakes … and 10,000,000,000 mosquitoes.

Mississippi: Come and feel better about you own state.

Missouri: Land of the big sky, the Unabomber, right-wing crazies, and Little Else.

Nebraska: Ask about our State Motto Contest.

Nevada: Hookers and poker.

New Hampshire: Go away and leave us alone.

New Jersey: You want a %$#*! motto? I got yer %$#* motto right here.

New Mexico: Lizards make excellent pets.

New York: You have the right to remain silent; you have the right to an attorney.

North Carolina: Tobacco is a vegetable.

North Dakota: We really are one of the 50 States.

Ohio: At least we're not Michigan.

Oklahoma: Like the play, only no singing.

Oregon: Spotted Owl … it's what's for dinner.

Pennsylvania: Cook with coal.

Rhode Island: We're not really an island.

South Carolina: Remember The Civil War? We didn't actually surrender.

South Dakota: Closer than North Dakota.

Tennessee: The Educashun State

Texas: Si' Hablo Ing'les (Yes, I speak English).

Utah: Our Jesus is better than your Jesus.

Vermont: Yep.

Virginia: Who says government stiffs and slackjaw yokels don't mix?

Washington: Help! We're overrun by Nerds and Slackers!

Washington, DC: Wanna be Mayor?

West Virginia: One big happy family … really!

Wisconsin: Come cut the cheese.

Wyoming: Where men are men … and the sheep are scared!

LORENA BOBBITT'S SISTER
ARRESTED IN CLEARWATER, FLORIDA!

Lorena Bobbitt's sister Luella was arrested yesterday for an alleged attempt to perform the same act on her husband as her famous sister had done several years ago. Sources reveal the sister was not as accurate as Lorena. She allegedly missed the target and stabbed her husband in the upper thigh causing severe muscle and tendon damage. The husband is reported to be in serious but stable condition. Luella has been arrested and charged with one count of mis de wiener.

(NO TITLE)

A young man married a beautiful woman who had previously divorced their husbands. On their wedding night she told her new husband, "Please be gentle, I'm still a virgin."

"What?" said the puzzled groom. "How can that be if you've been married ten times?"

"Well, husband #1 was a sales representative. He kept telling me how great it was going to be.

Husband #2 was in software services. He was never sure how it was supposed to function, but he said he'd look into it and get back to me.

Husband #3 was from field services. He said everything checked out diagnostically, but he just couldn't get the system up.

Husband #4 was in telemarketing. Every though he knew he had the order, he didn't know when he'd be able to deliver.

Husband #5 was an engineer. He understood the basic process perfectly, but wanted three years to research, implement and design a new state-of-the art method.

Husband #6 was from finance and administration. He thought he knew how, but he wasn't sure whether it was his job or not.

Husband #7 was in marketing. Although he had a product, he was never sure how to position it.

Husband #8 was a psychiatrist. All he ever did was talk about it.

Husband #9 was a gynecologist. All he did was look at it.

Husband #10 was a stamp collector. All he ever did was … God, I miss him!

But now that I've married you, I'm so excited!"

"Good," said the husband, "but, why?"

"You're a stock broker. This time I know I'm gonna get screwed!"

GOLF BALLS

A man entered the bus, with both of his front pant pockets full of golf balls, and sat down next to a blonde. The blonde kept looking quizzically at him and his bulging pockets. Finally, after many such glances from her, he said, "It's golf balls."

The blonde continued to look at him thoughtfully and finally asked, does it hurt as much as tennis elbow?"

HOLLYWOOD SQUARES

Peter Marshall was the host asking the questions, of course.

Q: Do female frogs croak?
A: Paul Lynde – If you hold their little heads under water long enough.

Q: If you're going to make a parachute jump, at least how high should you be?
A: Charley Weaver - Three days of steady drinking should do it.

Q: True or False, a pea can last as long as 5,000 years.
A: George Gobel – Boy, it sure seems that way sometimes.

Q: You've been having trouble going to sleep. Are you probably a man or a woman?
A: Don Knotts – That's what's been keeping me awake.

Q: According to Cosmo, if you meet a stranger at a party and you think he's attractive, is it okay to come out and ask him if he's married?
A: Rose Marie – No. wait until morning.

Q: Which of your five senses tends to diminish as you get older?
A: Charley Weaver – My sense of decency.

Q: In Hawaiian, does it take more than three words to say "I Love You"?
A: Vince Price – No, you can say it with a pineapple and a twenty.

Q: What are "Do It," "I Can Help," and "I Can't Get Enough"?
A: George Gobel – I don't know, but it's coming from the next apartment.

Q: As you grow older, do you tend to gesture more or less with your hands while talking?

A: Rose Marie – You ask me one more growing old question Peter, and I'll give you a gesture you'll never forget.

Q: Paul, why do Hell's Angels wear leather?
A: Because chiffon wrinkles too easily.

Q: Charley, you've just decided to grow strawberries. Are you going to get any during the first year?
A: Of course not, I'm too busy growing strawberries.

Q: In bowling, what's a perfect score?
A: Rose Marie – Ralph, the pin boy.

Q: It is considered in bad taste to discuss two subjects at nudist camps. One is politics, what is the other?
A: Paul Lynde – Tape measurers.

Q: During a tornado, are you safer in the bedroom or the closet?
A: Rose Marie – Unfortunately Peter, I'm always safe in the bedroom.

Q: Can boys join the Camp File Girls?
A: Marty Allen – Only after lights out.

Q: When you pat a dog on its head he will wag his tail. What will a goose do?
A: Paul Lynde – Make him bark?

Q: If you were pregnant for two years, what would you give birth to?
A: Paul Lynde – Whatever it is, it would never be afraid of the dark.

Q: According to Ann Landers, is there anything wrong with getting into the habit of kissing a lot of people?
A: Charley Weaver – It got me out of the army.

Q: While visiting China, your tour guide starts shouting "Poo! Poo! Poo!
   What does this mean?
A: George Gobel – Cattle Crossing.

Q: It is the most absurd and neglected part of your body, what is it?
A: Paul Lyned – Mine may be absurd but it certainly isn't neglected.

Q: Back in the old days, when Great Grandpa put horseradish on his head, what was he trying to do?
A: George Gobel – Get it in his mouth.

Q: Who stays pregnant for a longer period of time, your wife or your elephant?
A: Paul Lynde – Who told you about my elephant?

Q: When couples have a baby, who is responsible for its sex?
A: Charley Weaver – I'll lend him the car, the rest is up to him.

Q: Jackie Gleason recently revealed that he firmly believes in them and has actually seen them on at least two occasions. What are they?
A: Charley Weaver – His feet.

NEED SOME ARSENIC

So this woman walks into a pharmacy and asks the pharmacist for some arsenic. He asks "What for?"

She says "I want to kill my husband."

He says "Sorry, I can't do that."

She then reaches in her handbag a pulls out a photo of her husband in bed with the pharmacist's wife and hands it to him. He says, "You didn't tell me you had a prescription …"

RAISE IN SALARY

I, the Penis, hereby request a raise in salary for the following reasons.

1. I do physical labor.
2. I work at great depths.
3. I plunge head first into everything I do.
4. I do not get weekends or public holidays off.
5. I work in a damp environment.
6. I don't get paid overtime.
7. I work in a dark workplace that has poor ventilation.
8. I work in high temperatures, and my work exposes me to contagious diseases.

Dear Penis,
After assessing your request, and considering the arguments you have raised, the administration rejects your request for the following reasons:

1. You cannot work 8 hours straight.
2. You fall asleep on the job after brief work periods.
3. You do not always follow the orders of the management team.
4. You do not stay in your designated area and are often seen visiting other locations.
5. You do not take initiative – you need to be pressured and stimulated in order to start working.
6. You leave the workplace rather messy at the end of your shift.
7. You don't always observe necessary safety regulations, such as wearing the correct clothing.
8. You will retire well before you are 65.
9. You are unable to work double shifts.

10. You sometimes leave your designated work before you have completed the assigned task.

11. And if that were not enough, you have been seen constantly entering and exiting the workplace carry two suspicious looking bags.

Sincerely,
The Management.

GUESS WHICH ONE I'M GOING TO MARRY

A young Jewish man excitedly tells his mother he's falling in love and that he is going to get married. He says, "Just for fun, Ma, I'm going to bring over three women and you try and guess which one I'm going to marry."

The mother agrees.

The next day, he brings three beautiful women into the house and sits them down on the couch and they chat for a while.

He then says, "Okay, Ma, guess which one I'm going to marry."

She immediately replies, "The one on the right."

"That's amazing, Ma. You're right. How did you know?"

The Jewish mother replies, "I don't like her."

AIR SAFETY - SHIT HAPPENS

Air Safety thanks a retired Delta Captain for sending this "paraphrase" of a memorable safety PA from their Flight Attendants. In his own words....

I was flying to San Francisco from Seattle this weekend, and the flight attendant reading the flight safety information had the whole plane looking at each other like "what the heck?" (Getting Seattle people to look at each other is an accomplishment.) So once we got airborne, I took out my laptop and typed up what she said so I wouldn't forget. I've left out a few parts I'm sure, but this is most of it.

Before takeoff .... Hello and welcome to Alaska Flight 438 to San Francisco.

If you're going to San Francisco, you're in the right place. If you're not going to San Francisco, you're about to have a really long evening.

We'd like to tell you now about some important safety features of this aircraft. The most important safety feature we have aboard this plane is ... The Flight Attendants. Please look at one now.

There are 5 exits aboard this plane: 2 at the front, 2 over the wings, and one out the plane's real end. If you're seated in one of the exit rows, please do not store your bags by your feet. That would be a really bad idea.

Please take a moment and look around and find the nearest exit. Count the rows of seats between you and the exit. In the event that the needs arise to find one, trust me, you'll be glad you did. We have pretty blinking lights on the floor that will blink in the direction of the exits. White ones along the normal rows, and pretty red ones at the exit rows.

In the event of a loss of cabin pressure these baggy things will drop down over your head. You stick it over your nose and mouth like the flight attendant is doing now. The bag won't inflate, but there's oxygen there, promise. If you are sitting next to a small child, or someone who is acting like a small child, please do us all a favor and put on your mask first. If you are traveling with two or more children, please take a moment now to decide which one is your favorite. Help that one first, and then work your way down.

In the seat pocket in front of you is a pamphlet about the safety features of this plane. I usually use it as a fan when I'm having my own personal summer. It makes a very good fan. It also has pretty pictures. Please take it out and play with it now.

Please take a moment now to make sure your seat belts are fastened low and tight about your waist. To fasten the belt, insert the metal tab into the buckle. To release, it's a pulley thing - not a pushy thing like you car, because you're in an airplane – HELLO!!

There is no smoking in the cabin on this flight. There is also no smoking in the lavatories. If we see smoke coming from the lavatories, we will assume you are on fire and put you out. This is a free service we provide.

There are two smoking sections on this flight, one outside each wing exit. We do have a movie in the smoking sections tonight … hold on, let me check what it is … Oh here it is; the movie tonight is Gone with the Wind.

In a moment, we will be turning off the cabin lights, and it's going to get really dark, really fast. If you're afraid of the dark, now would be a good time to reach up and press the yellow button. The yellow button turns on your reading light. Please don't press the orange button unless you absolutely have to. The orange button is your seat ejection button.

We're glad to have you with us on board this flight. Thank you for choosing Alaska Air, and giving us your business and your money. If there's anything we can do to make you more comfortable, please don't hesitate to ask.

If you all weren't strapped down you would have given me a standing ovation, wouldn't you?

After landing ... Welcome to the San Francisco International Airport.

Sorry about the bumpy landing. It's not the captain's fault. It's not the copilot's fault. It's the Asphalt.

Please remain seated until the plane is parked at the gate. At no time in history has a passenger beaten a plane to the gate. So please don't even try.

Please be careful opening the overhead bins because "shit happens."

DEODORANT

A blonde walks into a pharmacy and asks the assistant for some rectum deodorant. The pharmacist, a little bemused, explains to the woman they don't sell rectum deodorant, and never have. Unfazed, the blonde assures the pharmacist that she has been buying the stuff from this store on a regular basis, and would like some more.

"I'm sorry," says the pharmacist, "we don't have any."

"But I always get it here," says the blonde.

"Do you have the container it comes in?" asks the pharmacist.

"Yes!", said the blond. "I'll go home and get it."

She returns with the container and hands it to the pharmacist who looks at it and says to her, "this is just a normal stick of underarm deodorant."

Annoyed, the blonde snatches the container back and reads it out loud from the container ... "To Apply, Push Up Bottom."

NEWSPAPER HEADLINES IN 2035

- White minorities still trying to have English recognized as California's third language.

- Spotted Owl plague threatens Northwestern United States' crops and livestock.

- Baby conceived naturally … scientist stumped.

- Last remaining Fundamentalist Muslim dies in the American Territory of the Middle East (formally known as Iran, Afghanistan, Syria, and Lebanon.)

- Iraq still closed off; physicists estimate it will take at least ten more years before radioactivity decreases to safe levels.

- Castro finally dies at age 112; Cuban cigars can now be imported legally, but President Chelsea Clinton had banned all smoking.

- George Z. Bush says he will run for President in 2036.

- Postal Service raises price of first class stamp to $17.89 and reduces mail delivery to Wednesday only.

- 35 year study: diet and exercise is the key to weight loss.

- Massachusetts executes last remaining conservative.

- Supreme Court rules punishment of criminals violates their civil rights.

- Upcoming NFL draft likely to focus on use of mutants.

- Average height of NBA players now nine feet, seven inches.

- Microsoft announces it has perfected its newest version of Windows so it crashes BEFORE installation is completed.

- News federal law requires that all nail clippers, screwdrivers, fly swatters, and rolled up newspapers must be registered by January 2036.

- Congress authorizes direct deposit of illegal political contributions to campaign accounts.

- Capital Hill intern indicted for refusing to have sex with congressman.

- IRS sets lowest tax rate at 75%.

- Average price of a single family home in Southern California is $2,500,000. A three bedroom apartment now rents for $8,000 a month.

- Celebrating Christmas now officially a felon as it offends too many people.

HOW MANY WOMEN

Q: How many women with MENOPAUSE does it take to change a light bulb?

A: One! ONLY ONE !!! And do you know why? Because no one else in this &^%#* house knows HOW to change a light bulb! They don't even know that a bulb is BURNED OUT! They would sit in the dark for THREE DAYS before they figured it out. And, once they figured it out, they wouldn't be able to find the light bulbs despite the fact that they've been in the SAME CUPBOARD for the past 17 YEARS! But if they did, by some miracle of God, actually find them 2 DAYS LATER, the chair they dragged to stand on to change the STUPID light bulb would STILL BE IN THE SAME SPOT!!!! AND UNDERNEATH IT WOULD BE THE WRAPPER THE STUPIT LIGHT BULBS CAME IN!!! BECAUSE NO ONE EVER CARRIES OUT THE GARBAGE!!!! IT'S A WONDER WE HAVEN'T ALL SUFFOCATED FROM THE PILES OF GARGAGE THAT ARE A FOOT DEEP THROUGHOUT THE ENTIRE HOUSE!!! IT WOULD TAKE AN ARMY TO CLEAN THIS &^%#(* HOUSE!
I'M SORRY …. What was the question?

LIFE EXPLAINED

On the first day God created the cow. God said, "You must go to the field with the farmer all day long and suffer under the sun, have calves and give milk to support the farmer. I will give you a life span of sixty years."

The cow said, "That's kind of a tough life you want me to live for sixty years. Let me have twenty and I'll give back the other forty." And God agreed.

On the second day God created the dog. Got said, "Sit all day by the door of your house and bark at anyone who comes in or walks past. I will give you a life span of twenty years."

The dog said, "That's too long to be barking. Give me ten years and I'll give you back the other ten." So God agreed (sigh).

On the third day God created the monkey. God said, "Entertain people, do monkey tricks, make them laugh. I'll give you a twenty year life span."

The monkey said, "How boring, monkey tricks for twenty years? I don't think so. Dog gave you back ten, so that's what I'll do too, okay?" And God agreed again.

On the fourth day God created man. God said, "Eat, sleep, lay, have sex, enjoy. Do nothing, just enjoy, enjoy. I'll give you twenty years."

Man said, "What? Only twenty years. No way man. Tell you what, I'll take my twenty years, ant the forty the cow gave back, and the ten the dog gave back and the ten the monkey gave back, that makes eighty, okay."

"Okay," said God. "You've got a deal."

So that is why the first twenty years we eat, sleep, play, have sex, enjoy, and do nothing; for the next forty years we slave in the sun to support our family; for the next ten years we do monkey tricks to entertain the grandchildren; and for the last ten years we sit on the front porch and bark at everyone.

Life has now been explained.

MARRIAGE (Part I)

Typical macho man married typical good-locking lady and after the wedding, he laid down the following rules: "I'll be home when I want, if I want and at what time I want – and I don't expect any hassle from you. I expect a great dinner to be on the table unless I tell you that I won't be home for dinner. I'll go hunting, fishing, boozing and card-playing when I want with my old buddies and don't you give me a hard time about it. Those are my rules. Any comments?"

His new bride said, "No, that's fine with me. Just understand that there will be sex here at seven o'clock every night whether you're here or not."

MARRIAGE (Part II)

Husband and wife had a bitter quarrel on the day of their 40th wedding anniversary. The husband yells, "When you die, I'm getting you a headstone that reads, "Here Lies My Wife – Cold As Ever!"

"Yeah?" she replies. "When you die, I'm getting you a headstone that reads, "Here Lies My Husband – Stiff At Last."

MARRIAGE (Part III)

Husband (a doctor) and his wife are having a fight at the breakfast table. Husband gets up in a rage and says, "And you are no good in bed either," and storms out of the house. After sometime he realizes he was nasty and decides to make amends and rings her up.

She comes to the phone after many rings and the irritated husband says,

"What took you so long to answer the phone?"

She says, "I was in bed."

"In bed this early, doing what?"

"Getting a second opinion!"

MARRIAGE (Part IV)

A man has six children and is very proud of his achievements. He is so proud of himself, that he starts calling his wife, "Mother of six" in spite of her objections. One night, they go to a party. The man decides that it's time to go home and wants to find out if his wife is ready to leave as well. He shouts at the top of his voice, "Shall we go home Mother of six?"

His wife, irritated by her husband's lack of discretion shouts right back, "Anytime you're ready, Father of four."

TOP OXYMORONS

Act naturally	Found missing	Resident alien
Advanced BASIC	Genuine imitation	Airline Food
Good grief	Same difference	Almost exactly
Government organization	Sanitary landfill	Alone together
Legally drunk	Silent scream	Living dead
Small crowd	Business ethics	Soft rock
Butt Head	Military Intelligence	Software documentation
New classic	Sweet sorrow	Childproof
"Now, then ..."	Synthetic natural gas	Passive aggression
Taped Live	Clearly misunderstood	Peace force
Extinct Life	Temporary tax increase	Computer jock
Plastic glasses	Terribly pleased	Computer security
Political science	Tight slacks	Definite maybe
Pretty ugly	Twelve-ounce pound cake	Diet ice cream
Working vacation	Exact estimate	Microsoft Works

THINGS TO PONDER

- Can you cry under water?

- How important does a person have to before they are considered assassinated instead of just murdered?

- If money doesn't grow on trees, then why do banks have branches?

- Since bread is square, then why is sandwich meat round?

- Why do you have to "put you two cents in" ... but it's only a "penny for your thoughts"? Where's that extra penny going to?

- Once you're in heaven, do you get stuck wearing the clothes you were buried in for eternity?

- Why does a round pizza come in a square box?

- What did cured ham actually have?

- How is it that we put man on the moon before we figured out it would be a good idea to put wheels on luggage?

- Why is it that people say they "sleep like a baby" when babies wake up every two hours?

- If a deaf person has to go to court, is it still called a hearing?

- If you drink Pepsi at work in the Coke factory, will they fire you?

- Why are you IN a movie, but you are ON TV?

- Why do people pay to go up tall buildings and then put money in binoculars to look at things on the ground?

- How come we choose from just two people for president and fifty for Miss America?

- Why do doctors leave the room while you change? They're going to see you naked anyway.

- Why is "bra" singular and "panties" plural?

SPEEDING TICKETS

A motorist was mailed a picture of his car speeding through an automated radar post in Harrisburg, PA. A $40 speeding ticket was included. Being cute, he sent the police department a picture of $40. The police responded with another mailed photo of handcuffs.

A young woman was pulled over for speeding. As the PA State Trooper walked to her car window, flipping open his ticket book, she said, "I bet you are going to sell me a ticket to the PA State Police Ball." He replied, "PA State Troopers don't have balls." There was a moment of silence while she smiled, and he realized what he'd just said. He then closed his book, got back in his patrol can and left. She was laughing too hard to start the car.

A young boy went up to his father and asked him, "Dad, what is the difference between potentially and realistically?"
The father thought for a moment, then answered, "Go as your mother if she would sleep with Robert Redford for a million dollars, and ask your sister if she would sleep with Brad Pitt for a million dollars, and ask your brother if he's sleep with Tom Cruise for a million dollars. Come back and tell me what you learn from that."
So the boy went to his mother and asked, "Would you sleep with Robert Redford for a million dollars?" The mother replied, "Of course I would! We could really use that money to fix up the house and send you kids to a great college!"
The boy then went to his sister and asked, "Would you sleep with Brad Pitt for a million dollars?" The girl replied, "Oh my God! I love Brad Pitt, I would sleep with him in a heartbeat, are you nuts?"
The boy then went to his brother and asked, "Would you sleep with Tom Cruise for a million dollars?" "Of course," The brother replied. "Do you know how much a million could buy?"
The boy pondered that for a few days, then went back to his dad. His father asked him. "Did you find out the difference between potentially and realistically?"
The boy replied. "Yes, sir. Potentially, we're sitting on three million dollars, but realistically, we're living with two sluts and a queer."

LOCAL NEWSPAPER NOTICES

- Free Yorkshire Terrier. Eight years old. Hateful little dog. Bites.

- Free Puppies: ½ cocker spaniel ½ sneaky neighbors' dog.

- Free Puppies: Part German Shepherd, part stupid dog.

- German Shepherd 85 lbs. Neutered. Speaks German. Free.

- Found: Dirty white dog. Looks like a rat … been out awhile … better be a reward.

- Snow blower for sale … only used on snowy days.

- Cows, calves never bred … also 1 gray bull for sale. $300 hardly used, call Chubby.

- Hummers – Largest selection ever – "If it's in stock, we have it!"

- Georgia Peaches, California grown – 89 cents lb.

- Nice Parachute: Never opened – used once.

- Tired of working for only $9.75 per hour? We offer profit sharing and flexible hours. Starting pay $7 - $9 per hour.

- Exercise Equipment: Queen size mattress & box springs - $175.

- Joining Nudist Colony! Must sell washer and dryer $300

- Open House: Body shapers toning salon. Free coffee and donuts.

KERMIT

A frog goes into a bank and approaches the teller. He can see from her nameplate that her name is Patricia Whack. "Miss Whack, I'd like to get a $30,000 loan to take a holiday." Patty looks at the frog in disbelief and asks his name. The frog says his name is Kermit Jagger, his dad is Mick Jagger, and that it's okay, he knows the bank manager.

Patty explains that he will need to secure the loan with come collateral. The frog says, "Sure. I have this," and produces a tiny porcelain elephant, about an inch tall, bright pink and perfectly formed. Very confused, Patty explains that she'll have to consult with the bank manager and disappears into a back office.

She finds the manager and says, "There's a frog called Kermit Jagger out there who claims to know you and wants to borrow $30,000, and he wants to use this as collateral." She holds up the tiny pink elephant. "I mean, what in the world is this?"

The bank manager looks back at her and says ... "It's a knickknack, Patty Whack. Give the frog a loan. His old man's a Rolling Stone."

(I bet you were all singing, right?)

MIRROR

A husband and wife are getting ready for bed. The wife is standing in front of a full length mirror taking a hard look at herself. "You know love" she says, "I look in the mirror and I see an old woman. My face is all wrinkled, my boobs are barely above my waist, my bum is hanging out a mile. I've got fat legs and my arms are all flabby." She turns to her husband and says .... "Tell me something positive to make me feel better about myself."

He thinks about it for a bit and then says in a soft voice, ... "well .... There's nothing wrong with your eyesight."

HAPPY HALLOWEEN Y'ALL

A bald man with a wooden leg gets invited to a HALLOWEEN PARTY. He doesn't know what costume to wear to hide hid head and his wooden leg, so he writes to a costume company to explain his problem. A few days later he received a parcel with the following note:

Dear Sir:
Please find enclosed a PIRATES OUTFIT. The spotted handkerchief will cover your bald head and, with your wooden leg, you will be just right as a pirate.
Very truly yours,
Acme Costume Co.

The man thinks this is terrible because they have emphasized his wooden leg and so he writes a letter of complaint. A week goes by and he received another parcel and a note, which says:

Dear Sir:
Please find enclosed a MONK'S HABIT. The long robe will cover your wooden leg and, with your bald head, you will really look the part.
Very truly yours,
Acme Costume Co.

Now the man is really upset since they have gone from emphasizing his wooden leg to emphasizing his bald head so again he writes the company another nasty letter of complaint. The following week he gets a small parcel and a note, which reads:

Dear Sir:
Please fin the enclosed bottle of MOLASSES. Pour the MOLASSES over your bald head, stick your wooden leg up your ass and go as a CARMEL APPLE!!!
Very truly yours,
Acme Costume Co.

THE ROBIN WILLIAMS PLAN

(Leave it to Robin Williams to come up with the perfect plan … what we need now is for our UN Ambassador to stand up and repeat this message.)

Robin Williams' plan … (Hard to argue with this logic!)

I see a lot of people yelling for peace but I have not heard of a plan for peace. So, here's one plan.

1. The US will apologize to the world for our "Interference" in their affairs, pas & present. You know, Hitler, Mussolini, Tojo, Noriega, Milosovich and the rest of those 'good ole boys.' We will never 'interfere" again.

2. We will withdraw our troops from all over the world, starting with Germany, South Korea and the Philippines. They don't want us there. We would station troops at our borders. No one sneaking through holes in the fence.

3. All illegal aliens have 90 days to get their affairs together and leave. We'll give them a free trip home. After 90 days the remainder will be gathered up and deported immediately. Regardless of who or where they are. France would welcome them.

4. All future visitors will be thoroughly checked and limited to 90 days unless given a special permit. No one from a terrorist nation would be allowed in. If you don't like it there, change it yourself and don't hide here. Asylum would never be available to anyone. We don't need any more cab drivers or 7-11 cashiers.

5. No "students" over age 21. The older ones are the bombers. If they don't attend classes, they get a "D" and it's back home baby.

6. The US will make a strong effort to become self-sufficient energy wise. This will include developing non-polluting sources of energy, but will require a temporary drilling of oil in the Alaskan wilderness. The caribou will have to cope for a while.

7. Offer Saudi Arabia and other oil producing countries $10 a barrel for their oil. If they don't like it, we go some place else. They can go somewhere else to sell their production. (About a week of the wells filling up the storage sites would be enough.)

8. If there is a famine or other natural catastrophe in the world, we will not "interfere." They can pray to Allah or whomever, for seeds, rain, cement or whatever they need. Besides most of what we give them is stolen or given to the army. The people who need it most get very little, if anything.

9. Ship the UN Headquarters to an isolated island some place. We don't need the spies and fair weather friends here. Besides, the building would make a good homeless shelter or lockup for illegal aliens.

10. All Americans must go to charm and beauty school. That way, no one can call us "Ugly Americans" any longer.

11. The language we speak is ENGLISH …. Learn it …. or LEAVE …

Now ain't that a winner of a plan. "The Statue of Liberty is no longer saying, 'Give me your poor, your tired, your huddled masses.' She's got a baseball bat and she's yelling, 'You want a piece of me?'"

MIND TEASERS OF COMMON KNOWLEDGE

There are 29 questions about things we see every day or have known about all our lives. How many can you get right? These little simple questions are harder that you think—it just shows you how little we pay attention to the common place things of life.

No cheating! No looking around!

Can you beat 20?? The average is 7. Answers at the bottom of the page.

1. On a standard traffic light, is the green on the top or bottom?
2. How many states are there?
3. In which hand is the Statue of Liberty' torch?
4. What six colors are on the classic Campbell's soup label?
5. What two letters don't appear on the telephone dial?
6. What two numbers on the telephone dial don't have letters by them?
7. When you walk does your left arm swing w/your right or left leg?
8. How many matches are in a standard pack?
9. On the United States flag is the top stripe red or white?
10. What is the lowest number on the FM dial?
11. Which way does water go down the drain, counter or clockwise?
12. Which way does a "no smoking" sign's slash run?
13. How many channels on a VHF TV dial?
14. Which side of a women's blouse are the buttons on?
15. On a NY license plate, is New York on the top or bottom?
16. Which way do fans rotate?
17. Whose face is on a dime?

18. How many sides does a stop sign have?

19. Do books have even-numbered pages on the right or left side?

20. How many lug nuts are on a standard car wheel?

21. How many sides are there on a standard pencil?

22. Sleepy, Happy, Sneezy, Grumpy, Dopey, Doc. Who's missing?

23. How many hot dog buns are in a standard package?

24. On which playing card is the card marker's trademark?

25. On which side of a Venetian blind is the cord that adjusts the opening between the slats?

26. On the back of a $1 bill, what is in the center?

27. There are 12 buttons on a touch tone phone. What two symbols bear no digits?

28. How many curves are there in the standard paper clip?

29. Does a merry-go-round turn counter or clockwise?

Answers: 1) Bottom 2) 50 3) Right 4) Blue, red, white, yellow, black, & gold 5) Q & Z 6) 1 & 0 7) Right 8) 20 9) Red 10) 88 11) counter (north of the equator) 12) Towards bottom right 13) 12 (no #1) 14) Left 15) Top 16) Clockwise as you look at it 17) Roosevelt 18) 8 19) Left 20) 5 21) 6 22) Bashful 23) 8 24) Ace of spades 25) Left 26) One 27) * , # 28) 3 29) Counter

25 SIGNS YOU'VE GROWN UP

1. Your potted plants are alive. And you can't smoke one of them.
2. Having sex in a twin-size bed is absurd.
3. You keep more food than beer in the fridge.
4. 6:00 AM is when you get up, not when you go to sleep.
5. You hear your favorite song on an elevator.
6. You carry an umbrella. You watch the Weather Channel.
7. Your friends marry and divorce instead of hookup and breakup.
8. You go from 130 days of vacation time to 7.
9. Jeans and a sweater no longer qualify as 'dressed up.'
10. You're the one calling the police because those darn kids next door don't know how to turn down the stereo.
11. Older relatives feel comfortable telling sex jokes around you.
12. You don't know what time Taco Bell closes anymore.
13. Your car insurance goes down and you car payments go up.
14. You feed your dog Science Diet instead of McDonald's.
15. Sleeping on the couch makes your back hurt.
16. You no longer take naps from noon to 6 PM.
17. Dinner and a movie = The whole date instead of the beginning of one.
18. Eating a basket of chicken wings at 3 AM would severely upset, rather than settle, your stomach.
19. You go to the drugstore for Ibuprofen and antacids, not condoms and pregnancy test kits.
20. A $4 bottle of wine is no longer 'pretty good stuff'.
21. You actually eat breakfast foods at breakfast time.
22. "I just can't drink the way I used to," replaces "I'm never going to drink that much again."

23. Over 90% of the time you spend in front of a computer is for real work.

24. You don't drink at home to save money before going to a bar.

25. You read this entire list looking for one sign that doesn't apply to you!

GOD IS WATCHING

Children were lined up in the cafeteria of a Catholic school for lunch. At the head of the table was a large pile of apples. The nun made a note, "Take only one, God is watching."

Moving through the line, at the other end of the table was a large pile of chocolate chip cookies. A boy wrote a note, "Take all you want, God is watching the apples."

CUTBACKS

The NFL announced today that for financial reasons they had to eliminate one team from the league. So they've decided to combine the Green Bay Packers and the Tampa Bay Buccaneers and form one team, therefore saving jobs. They will be known as the TAMPACKS.

Unfortunately, they're only good for one period and have no second string.

SNAPPY ANSWERS

A flight attendant was stationed at the departure gate to check tickets. As a man approached, she extended her hand for the ticket and he opened his trench coat and flashed her. Without missing a beat she said "Sir, I need to see your ticket, not your stub."

A lady was picking through the frozen turkeys at the grocery store, but couldn't find one big enough for her family. She asked a stock boy, "Do these turkeys get any bigger?" The stock boy replied, "No ma'am, they're dead."

The cop got out of his car and the kid who was stopped for speeding rolled down his window. "I've been waiting for you all day," the cop said. The kid replied, "Yeah, well I got here as fast as I could." When the cop finally stopped laughing, he sent the kid on his way without a ticket.

A truck driver was driving along on the freeway. A sign comes up that reads "low bridge ahead." Before he knows it the bridge is right ahead of him and he gets stuck under the bridge. The cop gets out of his car and walks around the truck driver, puts his hands on his hips and says, "Got stuck, huh?" The truck driver says, "No, I was delivering this bridge and ran out of gas."

A college teacher reminds her class of tomorrow's final exam. "Now class, I won't tolerate any excuses for you not being here tomorrow. I might consider a nuclear attack or a serious personal injury or illness, or a death in your immediate family but that's it, no other excuses whatsoever! A smart-ass guy in the back of the room raised his hand and asks, "What would you say if tomorrow I said I was suffering from complete and utter sexual exhaustion?" The entire class does its best to stifle their laughter and snickering. When silence is restored, the teacher smiles sympathetically at the student, shakes her head, and sweetly says, "Well, I guess you'd have to write the exam with your other hand."

CHRISTMAS SYMBOLS

Three med died in an accident after an office Christmas party and were met by Saint Peter at the pearly gates.

"In honor of this holy season," Saint Peter said, "You must each possess something that symbolizes Christmas to get into heaven."

The first man fumbled through his pockets and pulled out a lighter. He flicked it on. It represents a candle, he said. "You may pass through the pearly gates," Saint Peter said.

The second man reached into his pocket and pulled out a set of keys. He shook them and said, "They're bells." Saint Peter said you may pass through the pearly gates.

The third man started searching desperately through his pockets and finally pulled out a pair of women's panties. Saint Peter looked at the man with a raised eyebrow and asked, "And just what do those symbolize?" The man replied, "They're Carols."

JUST STOP IN FOR A DRINK AFTER WORK
(NO TITLE)

Two hillbillies from Tennessee walk into the local bar to wash the dust from their throats and grab a beer. They stand at the bar, drinking a beer and talking about current cattle prices. Suddenly, a woman at the nearby table, who is eating a sandwich, begins to cough.
After a minute or so, it becomes apparent that she is in real distress. One of the hillbillies looks at her and says, "Kin ya swaller?" The woman shakes her head no. "Kin ya breath?"

The woman begins to turn blue and shakes her head. The Hillbilly walks over to the woman. Lifts up the back of her dress, yanks down her panties, and runs his tongue all over her butt cheeks in a circular motion. The woman is so shocked, that she has a violent spasm and the obstruction flies out of her mouth.

As she begins to breath again, the hillbilly walks slowly back to the bar and takes a drink from his beer. His partner says, "Ya know, I'd heard about that there 'Hind Lick' maneuver, but I ain't never seen nobody do it."

HOTEL BILL

Next time you think your hotel bill is too high ... you might want to use this logic ...

A husband and wife are traveling by car from Key West to Boston. After almost twenty-four hours on the road, they're too tired to continue, and they decide to stop for a rest. They stop at a nice hotel and take a room, but they only plan to sleep for four hours and then get back on the road.

When they check out four hours later, the desk clerk hands them a bill for $350. The man explodes and demands to know why the charge is so high. He tells the clerk although it's a nice hotel, the rooms certainly aren't worth $350. When the clerk tells him $350 is the standard rate, the man insists on speaking to the Manager.

The Manager appears, listens to the man, and then explains that the hotel has an Olympic-sized pool and a huge conference center that were available for the husband and wife to use. "But we didn't use them," the man complains...

"Well, they are here, and you could have," explains the Manager. He goes on to explain they could have taken in one of the shows for which the hotel is famous. "The best entertainers from New York, Hollywood and Las Vegas perform here," the Manager says.

"But we didn't go to any of those shows," complains the man again.

"Well, we have them, and you could have", the Manager replies.

No matter what facility the Manager mentions, the man replies, "But we didn't use it."

The Manager is unmoved, and eventually the man gives up and agrees to pay. He writes a check and gives it to the Manager. The

Manager is surprised when he looks at the check. "But sir" he says, "This check is only made for $100."

"That's right," says the man. "I charged you $250 for sleeping with my wife."

"But I didn't!" exclaims the Manager.

"Well," the man replies, "she was there, and you could have."

BUMPER STICKERS YOU WOULD LIKE TO SEE

- Impotence … Nature's way of saying "No hard feelings."

- The proctologist called .., they found your head.

- Everyone has a photographic memory … some just don't have any film.

- Save your breath … You'll need it to blow up your date.

- Your ridiculous little opinion has been noted.

- I used to have a handle on life … but it broke off.

- WANTED: Meaningful overnight relationship.

- Guys … just because you have one, doesn't mean you have to be one.

- Some people just don't know how to drive … I call these people "Everybody But Me."

- Heart Attacks … God's revenge for eating His animal friends.

- Don't like my driving? Then quit watching me.

- If you can read this … I can slam on my breaks and sue you.

- Some people are only alive because it is illegal to shoot them.

- Try not to let your mind wander … It is too small and fragile to be out by itself.

- Hang up and drive!!

- Welcome to America … now speak English.

- Jesus loves you … but everyone else thinks you are an ass.

LOVE STORY

I shall seek and find you ...
I shall take you to bed and have my way with you ...
I will make you ache, shake and sweat until you moan and groan.
I will make you beg for mercy ... beg for me to stop.
I will exhaust you to the point that you will be relieved when I'm finished with you.
And you will be weak for days.
All My Love,
The FLU

EXCERPTS FROM A DOG'S DAILY DIARY

8:00 AM	Oh boy! Dog food! My favorite!
9:30 AM	Oh boy! A car ride! My favorite!
9:40 AM	Oh boy! A walk! My favorite!
10:30 AM	Oh boy! A car ride! My favorite!
11:30 AM	Oh boy! Dog food! My favorite!
12:00 PM	Oh boy! The kids! My favorite!
1:00 PM	Oh boy! The yard! My favorite!
4:00 PM	Oh boy! The kids! My favorite!
5:00 PM	Oh boy! Dog food! My favorite!
5:30 PM	Oh boy! Mum! My favorite!
6:00 PM	Oh boy! Playing ball! My favorite!
6:30 PM	Oh boy! Sleeping in master's bed! My favorite!

EXCERPTS FROM A CAT'S DAILY DIARY

My captors continue to taunt me with bizarre little dangling objects. They dine lavishly on fresh meat, while I am forced to eat dry cereal. The only thing that keeps me going is the hope of escape, and the mild satisfaction I get from ruining the occasional piece of furniture.

Tomorrow I may eat another houseplant. Today my attempt to kill my captors by weaving around their feet while they were walking almost succeeded; must try this at the top of the stairs.

In an attempt to disgust and repulse these vile oppressors, I once again induced myself to vomit on their favorite chair; must try this on their bed.

Decapitated a mouse and brought them the headless body, in attempt to make them aware of what I am capable of, and to try to strike fear into their hearts. They only cooed and condescended about what a good little cat I was. Hmmm, not working according to plan.

There was some sort of gathering of their accomplices. I was placed in solitary throughout the event. However, I could hear the noise and smell the food. More importantly, I overheard that my confinement was due to MY power of "allergies." Must learn what this is and how to use it to my advantage.

I am convinced the other captives are flunkies and maybe snitches. The dog is routinely released and seems more than happy to return. He is obviously a half-wit.

The bird on the other hand has got to be an informant, and speaks with them regularly. I am certain he reports my every move. Due to his current placement in the metal room, his safety is assured. But I can wait; it is only a matter of time....

THINGS THAT SOUND DIRTY AT CHRISTMAS, BUT AREN'T

1. Did you get any under the tree?
2. I think you balls are hanging too low.
3. Check out Rudolph's Honker!
4. Santa's sack is really bulging.
5. Lift up the skirt so I can get a clean breath.
6. Did you get a piece of the fruitcake?
7. I love licking the end till it's really sharp and pointy.
8. From here you can't tell if they're artificial or real.
9. Can I interest you in some dark meat?
10. To get it to stand up straight, try propping it against the wall.

LOGIC IN ACTION

A man walks into a pharmacy and wanders up and down the aisles. The sales girl notices him and asks him if she can help him

He answers that he is looking for a box of tampons for his wife. She directs him down the correct aisle.

A few minutes later, he deposits a huge bag of cotton balls and a ball of string on the counter. She says, confused, "Sir, I thought you were looking for some tampons for your wife?"

He answers, "You see, it's like this. Yesterday, I sent my wife to the store to get me a carton of cigarettes, and she came back with a tin of tobacco and some rolling papers; cause it's sooooooooooooo much cheaper. So ... I figure if I have to roll my own ...... so does she."

THE STORY OF ONESTONE THE INDIAN BRAVE

This was his Indian name given to him because he had only one testicle. After years and years of this torment Onestone cracked and said, "If anyone calls me Onestone again, I will kill them!"

The word got around and nobody called him that any more.

Then one day a young girl named Blue Bird forgot and said, "Good morning Onestone."

He jumped up, grabbed her and took her deep into the forest there he shagged her all day, he shagged her all night, he shagged her all the next day, until Blue Bird died from exhaustion.

The word got around that Onestone meant business.

Years went by until a woman named Yellow Bird returned to the village after many years away. Yellow Bird who was Blue Bird's cousin was overjoyed when she saw Onestone and hugged him and said, "Good to see you Onestone."

Onestone grabbed her and took her deep into the forest where he shagged her all day, shagged her all night, shagged her all the next day, shagged her all the next night, but Yellow Bird wouldn't die!

What's the moral of the story? This is great!

You can't kill two birds with one stone.

BLONDES

Two factory workers, a man and a woman, were talking. "I know how to get some time off from work," said the man.

"How?" asked the blonde.

"Watch," the man replied. He proceeded to climb up to the rafters, then hung upside down from them.

The boss walked in, saw the worker hanging from the ceiling, and asked, "What on earth are you doing?"

"I'm a light bulb," answered the guy.

"I think you need some time off," said the boss.

So the man jumped down and walked out of the factory.

The blonde began walking out, too. The boss asked her, "Where do you think you're going?"

"Home," she replied. "I can't work in the dark."

TWO WEEKS BEFORE CHRISTMAS

T'was two weeks before Christmas, And all through Iraq,
The people still worried that Saddam would be back.
The soldiers went out on their nightly patrol,
Capturing the bad guys was always their goal!

With raids seeming endless in the triangle Sunni,
We hoped that not all of Iraq was so looney!
We gathered the tribe of Saddam, in Tikrit,
And suddenly now they all started to snit!

They told of a farm where Hussein just might be
Odierno then called on our boys – from the great 4th ID!
More rapid than Baathists our soldiers they came,
And he whistled and shouted and called them by name.

Now Delta, Now Rangers, Now Calvary, too!
On Green Hats, on Pilots, I need all of you!
Go to that farm and secure it right now!
Capture his ass – you guys know how!

Off went our soldiers under cover of night,
So stealthy, so quiet with no trace of light
While we back at home were eating our lunches,
Our boys on the ground were following hunches!

And then it was time for the raid to begin.
The first target came up – empty within!
Could it be our Intel was wrong once again?
No! Somewhere nearby is the wolf in his den!

And then, in a twinkling, camouflage torn away
In a hole in the ground did their quarry lay.
Dazed and confused, right at them he looked,
Did the stupid old fool know his goose was now cooked?

He dressed all in rags from his toes to his head,
And his beard was a matted as 12 day-old bread!
How the mighty had fallen, could this be Hussein?
One look in his eyes was to know he's insane!

Our boys got their man – how proud we all are
The relief in our country is felt near and afar
A bath he had had now – yet he'll never be clean
Forever tinted with mass torture and his Fedaheen.

To our soldiers we give our undying respect
You always give more than we ever expect
We hope you can have now a night with some fun
Your loved ones back home say – JOB DAMN WELL DONE!

A LITTLE HOLIDAY FACT

According to the Alaska Department of Fish and Game, while both male and female reindeer grow antlers in the summer each year, male reindeer drop their antlers at the beginning of winter, usually late November to mid December. Female reindeer retain their antlers till after they give birth in the spring. Therefore, according to every historical rendition depicting Santa's reindeer, every single one of them, from Rudolph to Blitzen – had to be a girl. Only women, while pregnant, would be able to drag a fat man in a red velvet suit all around the world in one night and not get lost.

JOB APPLICATION

This is an actual job application that a 17-year old boy submitted at a McDonald's restaurant in Florida, and they hired him because he was so honest and funny.

NAME: Greg Bulmash

SEX: Not yet. Still waiting for the right person.

DESIRED POSITION: Company's President or Vice President. But seriously, whatever's available. If I was in a position to be picky, I wouldn't be applying here in the first place.

DESIRED SALARY: $185,000 a year plus stock options and a Michael Ovitz severance package. If that's not possible, make an offer and we can haggle.

EDUCATION: Yes

LAST POSITION HELD: Target for middle management hostility.

SALARY: Less than I'm worth.

MOST NOTABLE ACHIEVEMENT: My incredible collection of stolen pens and post-it notes.

REASON FOR LEAVING: It sucked.

AVAILABLE TO WORK: Of course! That's why I'm applying.

PREFERENCE HOURS: 1:30 – 3:30 PM, Monday, Tuesday and Thursday.

DO YOU HAVE ANY SPECIAL SKILLS?: Yes, but they're better suited to a more intimate environment.

MAY WE CONTACT YOUR CURRENT EMPLOYER: If I had one, would I be here?

DO YOU HAVE A CAR: I think the more appropriate question here would be "Do you have a car that runs?"

HAVE YOU RECEIVED ANY SPECIAL AWARDS OR RECOGNITIONS: I may already be a winner of the Publishers Clearing House Sweepstakes.

DO YOU SMOKE: On the job, no; on my breaks, yes.

WHAT WOULD YOU LIKE TO BE DOING IN FIVE YEARS: Living in the Bahamas with a fabulously wealthy dumb blonde super model who thinks I'm the greatest thing since sliced bread. Actually, I'd like to be doing that now.

DO YOU CERTIFY THAT THE ABOVE IS TRUE AND COMPLETE TO THE BEST OF YOUR KNOWLEDGE: Yes.

SIGN HERE: Aries.

IN HONOR OF STUPID PEOPLE

In case you needed further proof that the human race is doomed through stupidity, here are some actual label instructions on consumer goods.

- On a Sears hairdryer: Do not use while sleeping.

- On a bag of Fritos: You could be a winner! No purchase necessary. Details inside.

- On a bar of Dial soap: "Directions: Use like regular soap."

- On some Swanson frozen dinners: "Serving suggestions: Defrost."

- On Tesco's Tiramisu dessert (printed on bottom): "Do not turn upside down."

- On Marks K& Spencer Bread Pudding: "Product will be hot after heating."

- On packaging for a Rowenta iron: "Do not iron clothes on body."

- On Boot's Children Cough Medicine: "Do not drive a car or operate machinery after taking this medication."

- On Nytol Sleep Aid: "Warning: May cause drowsiness."

- On most brands of Christmas lights: "For indoor or outdoor use only."

- On a Japanese food processor: "Not to be used for the other use."

- On Sainsbury's peanuts: "Warning: contains nuts."

- On an American Airlines packet of nuts: "Instructions: Open packet, eat nuts."

- On a child's superman costume: "Wearing of this garment does not enable you to fly."

- On a Swedish chainsaw: "Do not attempt to stop chain with your hands or genitals."

THIS IS A GREAT TIP FOR YOUR NEXT HOSPITAL STAY

A sweet grandmother telephoned Mount Sinai Hospital. She timidly asked, "Is it possible to speak to someone who can tell me how a patient is doing?"

The operator said, "I'll be glad to help, Dear. What's the name and room number?"

The grandmother in her weak tremulous voice said, "Holly Finkel in room 302."

The Operator replied, "Let me check. Oh, good news. Her records say that Holly is doing very well. Her blood pressure is fine; her blood work just came back as normal and her physician, Dr. Cohen, has scheduled her to be discharged Tuesday."

The Grandmother said, "Thank you. That's wonderful! I was so worried! God bless you for the good news."

The operator replied, "You're more than welcome. Is Holly your daughter?"

The Grandmother said, "No, I'm Holly Finkel in 302. No one tells me shit."

A POEM FOR COMPUTER USERS OVER 40

A computer was something on TV
From a science fiction show of note;
A window was something you hated to clean,
And ram was the cousin of a goat.

Meg was the name of my girlfriend;
And gig was a job for the night'
Now they all mean different things,
And that really mega bites.

An application was for employment;
A program was a TV show;
A cursor used profanity;
A keyboard was a piano.

Memory was something that you lost with age;
A CD was a bank account;
And if you had a 3-inch floppy,
You hoped nobody found out.

Compress was something you did to the garbage,
Not something you did to a file;
And if you unzipped anything in public,
You'd be in jail for a while.

Log on was adding wood to the fire;
Hard drive was a long trip on the road;
A mouse pad was where a mouse lived;
And backup happened to your commode.

Cut you did with a pocket knife;
Paste you did with glue;
A web was a spider's home,
And a virus was the flu.

I guess I'll stick to my pad and paper
And the memory is my head;
I hear nobody's been killed in a computer crash,
But when it happens, they wish they were dead.

THE NEW SUPERMARKET

The new supermarket near our house has an automatic water mister to keep the produce fresh. Just before it goes on, you hear the sound of distant thunder and the smell of fresh rain. When you approach the milk case, you hear cows mooing and witness the scent of fresh hay. When you approach the egg case, you hear hens cluck and cackle and the air is filled with the pleasing aroma of bacon and eggs frying. The veggie department features the smell of fresh buttered corn. But, I don't buy toilet paper there any more.

BEST SEEN SIGNS

- On the trucks of a local plumbing company in NE Pennsylvania: "Don't sleep with a drip. Call your plumber."

- At a tire shop in Milwaukee: "Invite us to your next blowout."

- Door of a plastic surgeon's office: "Hello, Can we pick your nose or would you rather do it."

- At a laundry shop: "How about we refund your money, send you a new one at no charge, close the store and have the manager shot. Would that be satisfactory?"

- At a towing company: "We don't charge an arm and a leg. We want tows."

- On an electrician's truck: "Let us remove your shorts."

- In a non-smoking area: "If we see smoke, we will assume you are on fire and take appropriate action."

- At an optometrist office: "If you don't see what you're looking for, you've come to the right place."

- On a taxidermist's window: "We really know our stuff."

- On a fence: "Salesmen welcome! Dog food is expensive."

- At a car dealership: "The best way to get back on your feet – miss a car payment."

- Outside a muffler shop: "No appointment necessary. We'll hear you coming."

- In a veterinarian's waiting room: "Be back in 5 minutes. Sit! Stay!"

- On a maternity room door: "Push. Push. Push."

- In a podiatrist's office: "Time wounds all heels."

- At a radiator shop (A-1 Radiator): "Best Place in Town to take a Leak."

MID-LIFE VIEWS FROM LADIES

1. Mid-life is when the growth of hair on our legs shows down. This gives us plenty of time to care for our newly acquired mustache.

2. Mid-life is when you can stand naked in front of a mirror and you can see your rear without turning around

3. Mid-life is when you go for a mammogram and you realize that this is the only time someone will ask you to appear topless.

4. Mid-life is when you want to grab every firm young lovely in a tube top and scream, "Listen honey, even the Roman empire fell and those will too."

5. Mid-life brings wisdom to know that life throws us curves and we're sitting on our biggest ones.

6. Mid-life is when you look at your-know-it-all, beeper wearing teenager and think: "For this I have stretch marks?"

7. In mid-life your memory starts to go. In fact the only thing we can retain is water.

8. Mid-life means that your Body by Jake now includes Legs by Rand McNally...more red and blue lines than an accurately scaled map of Wisconsin.

9. Mid-life means that you become more reflective...You start pondering the "big" questions. What is life? Why am I here? How much Healthy Choice ice cream can I eat before it's no longer a healthy choice?

10. Maybe our bodies simply have to expand to hold all the wisdom and love we've acquired. That's my philosophy and I'm sticking to it!

GREAT BUMPER STICKERS

- If you can't feed em, don't breed em!

- Constipated People Don't Give a Crap.

- If You Can Read This, I've Lost My Trailer.

- Horn Broken…Watch for Finger.

- The Earth Is Full – Go Home.

- I Have The Body Of A God – Buddha.

- So Many Pedestrians – So Little Time.

- Cleverly Disguised As A Responsible Adult.

ONLY IN KENTUCKY

- The owner of a golf course in Kentucky was confused about paying an invoice, so he decided to ask his secretary for some mathematical help. He called her into his office and said, "You graduated from The University of Kentucky and I need some help. If I were to give you $20,000, minus 14%, how much would you take off?" The secretary thought a moment, then replied, "Everything but my earnings."

- A group of Kentucky friends went deer hunting and paired off in twos for the day. That night, one of the hunters returned alone, staggering under the weight of an eight-point buck. "Where's Henry?" the others asked. "Henry had a stroke of some kind. He's a couple of miles back up the trail." The successful hunter replied. "You left Henry laying out there and carried the deer back?" they inquired. "A tough call," nodded the hunter. "But I figured no one is going to steal Henry!"

- A senior at Kentucky was overheard saying…"When the end of the world comes, I hope to be in Kentucky." When asked why, he replied he'd rather be in Kentucky because everything happens in Kentucky 20 years later than in the rest of the civilized world.

- The young man from Kentucky came running into the store and said to his buddy, "Bubba, somebody just stole your pickup truck from the parking lot!" Bubba replied, "Did you see who it was?" The young man answered, "I couldn't tell, but I got the license plate number."

SOME THINGS ARE SACRED DAMMIT!

On the 2nd tee of the golf course with his wife, the husband says, "Twenty years ago I had a brief affair, it meant nothing. I hope you can forgive me." His wife was hurt, but said, "Dearest, those days are long gone. What we have now is far more valuable. I forgive you." They embraced and kissed.

On the 17th tee, the husband was starting his back swing when the wife blurted out, "I'm sorry darling, I've been so conscience-stricken since you told me of your affair. Since we're being honest with each other, I have something to tell you also. Thirty-two years ago I had a sex change operation. I was a man before I met you. I hope you can forgive me.

The husband froze in the top of his back swing, and then threw a fit! He slammed the driver into the ground, kicked the ball into the woods, stormed off the tee, pushed the golf cart over on its side, broke the rest of his clubs one by one, then started on hers. He screamed and ranted. "You liar! You cheat! You despicable deceiver! How could you? I trusted you with all my heart and soul...and all these years you've been playing off the ladies tees!"

THE OLDER GENERATION

An elderly gentleman (mid nineties); very well dressed, hair will groomed, great looking suit, flower in his lapel smelling slightly of a good after shave, presenting a well looked-after image, walks into an upscale cocktail lounge. Seated at the bar is an elderly looking lady (mid eighties). The gentleman walks over, sits alongside of her, orders a drink, takes a sip, turns to her and says, "So tell me, do I come here often?"

An elderly gentleman had serious hearing problems for a number of years. He went to the doctor and the doctor was able to have him fitted for a set of hearing aids that allowed him to hear 100%. He went back in a month and the doctor said, "Your hearing is perfect. Your family must be really pleased that you can hear again." The gentleman replied, "Oh, I haven't told my family yet. I just sit around and listen to the conversations. I've changed my will three times!"

Two elderly gentlemen from a retirement center were sitting on a bench under a tree when one turned to the other and said: "Slim, I'm 83 years old now and I'm just full of aches and plains. I know you're about my age. How do you feel?"
Slim said, "I feel just like a newborn baby."
"Really? Like a newborn baby?"
"Yep, no hair, no teeth, and I think I just wet my pants."

A man was telling his neighbor, "I just bought a new hearing aid. It cost me four thousand dollars, but its state of the art. It's perfect.
"Really," answered the neighbor. "What kind is it?"
"Twelve thirty," he replied.

An elderly couple had dinner at another couple's house, and after eating, the wives left the table and went into the kitchen. The two gentlemen were talking, and one said, "Last night we went out to a new restaurant and it was really great. I would recommend it very highly."
The other man said, "What is the name of the restaurant?"

The first man thought and thought and finally said, "What is the name of that flower and give to someone you love? You know...the one that's red and has thorns."

"Do you mean a rose?"

"Yes, that's the one," replied the man. He then turned towards the kitchen and yelled, "Rose, what's the name of that restaurant we went to last night?"

Three elderly men are out walking. First one says, "Windy, isn't it?"
Second one says, "No, it's Thursday!"
Third one says, "So am I. Let's go get a beer."

An 82 year-old man went to the doctor to get a physical. A few days later, the doctor saw Maurice walking down the street with a gorgeous young woman on his arm. A couple days later, the doctor called Maurice and said, "You're really doing great, aren't you?"

Maurice replied, "Just doing what you said, Doc: 'Get a hot mamma and be cheerful.'"

"I didn't say that...I said, 'You've got a heart murmur; be careful.'"

WHEN I SAY I'M BROKE...I'M BROKE

A little old lady answered a knock on the door one day, only to be confronted by a well-dressed young man carrying a vacuum cleaner. "Good morning," said the young man. "If I could take a couple of minutes of your time, I would like to demonstrate the very latest in high-powered vacuum cleaners."

"Go away!" said the old lady, "I haven't got any money!" and she proceeded to close the door. Quick as a flash, the young man wedged his foot in the door and pushed it wide open.

"Don't be too hasty!" he said. "Not until you have at least seen my demonstration." And with that, he emptied a bucket of horse manure onto her hallway carpet. "If this vacuum cleaner does not remove all traces of this horse manure from your carpet, Madam, I will personally eat the remainder.

The old lady stepped back and said, "Well I hope you've got a darned good appetite, because they cut off my electricity this morning. What part of broke do you not understand?"

WARNING LABELS ON LIQUOR BOTTLES

The following warning labels should be placed on all varieties of alcohol containers as a public service by the liquor manufacturers:

1. WARNING: This consumption of alcohol man leave you wondering what the hell happened to your bra and panties.
2. WARNING: The consumption of alcohol may make you think you are whispering when you are not.
3. WARNING: The consumption of alcohol is a major factor in dancing like a retard.
4. WARNING: The consumption of alcohol may cause you to tell your friends over and over again that you love them.
5. WARNING: The consumption of alcohol may cause you to think you can sing.
6. WARNING: The consumption of alcohol may lead you to believe that ex-lovers are dying for you to telephone them at four in the morning.
7. WARNING: The consumption of alcohol may make you think you can logically converse with members of the opposite sex without spitting.
8. WARNING: The consumption of alcohol may create the illusion that you are tougher, smarter, faster and better looking than most people.
9. WARNING: The consumption of alcohol may lead you to think people are laughing WITH you.
10. WARNING: The consumption of alcohol may cause pregnancy.
11. WARNING: The consumption of alcohol may be a major factor in getting your butt kicked.
12. WARNING: The consumption of alcohol may Mack you tink you kan type reel gode.

XMAS SYMBOLS

Three men died in an accident after an office Christmas party and were met by Said Peter at the pearly gates.

"In honor or this holy season, "Saint Peter said, "You must each possess something that symbolizes Christmas to get into heaven."

The first man fumbled through his pockets and pulled out a lighter. He flicked it on. It represents a candle, he said. "You may pass through the pearly gates," Saint Peter said.

The second man reached into his pocket and pulled out a set of keys, He shook them and said, "They're bells". Saint Peter said you may pass through the pearly gates.

The third man started searching desperately through his pockets and finally pulled out a pail of women's panties. Saint Peter looked at the man with a raised eyebrow and asked, "And just what do those symbolize?" The man replied, "They're Carols."

2004

ANDY ROONEY

Comments made on "60 Minutes":

- I like big cars, big boats, big motorcycles, big houses and big campfires. I believe the money I make belongs to me and my family, not some government stooge with a bad comb-over who wants to give it away to crack addicts for squirting out babies.

- Guns do not make you a killer. I think killing makes you a killer. You can kill someone with a baseball bat or a car, but no one is trying to ban you from driving to the ball game.

- I believe they are called the Boy Scouts for a reason. That is why there are no girls allowed. Girls belong in the Girl Scouts! ARE YOU LISTENING MARTHA BURKE?

- I think that if you feel homosexuality is wrong, it is not a phobia, it is an opinion.

- I don't think being a minority makes you a victim of anything except numbers. The only things I can think of that are truly discriminatory are things like the United Negro College Fund, Jet Magazine, Black Entertainment Television and Miss Black America.

- Try to have things like the United Caucasian College Fund, Cloud Magazine, White Entertainment Television, or Miss White America; and see what happens. Jesse Jackson will be knocking down your door.

- I have the right "NOT" to be tolerant of others because they are different, weird, or tick me off. When 70% of the people who get arrested are black, in cities where 70% of the population is black, that is not racial profiling. It is the Law of Probability.

- I believe that if you are selling me a milk shake, a pack of cigarettes, a newspaper or a hotel room, you must do it in English! As a matter of fact, if you want to be an American citizen, you should have to speak English!

- My father and grandfather didn't die in vain so you can leave the countries you were born in to come over and disrespect ours.

- I think the police should have every right to shoot your sorry self if you threaten them after they tell you to stop. If you can't understand the word "freeze" or "stop" in English, see the above lines.

- I don't think just because you were not born in this country, you are qualified for any special loan programs, government sponsored bank loans or tax breaks, etc., so you can open a hotel, coffee shop, trinket store, or any other business.

- We did not go to the aid of certain foreign countries and risk our lives in wars to defend their freedoms, so that decades later they could come over here and tell us our constitution is a living document; and open to their interpretations.

- I believe a self-righteous liberal or conservative with a cause is more dangerous than a Hell's Angel with an attitude.

- I think Bill Gates has every right to keep every penny he made and continue to make more. If it ticks you off, go and invent the next operating system that's better, and put your name on the building. Ask your buddy who invented the Internet to help you.

- I think tattoos and piercing are fine if you want them, but please don't pretend they are a political statement. And, please, stay home until that new lip ring heals. I don't want to look at your ugly infected mouth as you serve me French fries!

- I am sick of "Political Correctness." I know a lot of black people, and not a single one of them was born in Africa; so how can they be "African Americans"? Besides, Africa is a continent. I don't go around saying I am a European-American because my great, great, great, great, great grandfather was from Europe.

- I am proud to be from America and nowhere else. And if you don't like my point of view, tough. DON'T PASS IT ON!!

- While life may not be the party we hoped for, while we're here we might as well dance.

BILL GATES DIES AND FACES GOD

"Well, Bill," said God, "I'm really confused on this one. I'm not sure whether to send you to Heaven or Hell! After all, you helped society enormously by putting a computer in almost every home in the world and yet you created that awful Windows. I'm going to do something I've never done before. I'm going to let you decide where you want to go!"

Mr. Gates replied: "Well, thanks, Lord. What's the difference between the two?"

God said: "You can take a peek at both places briefly if it will help you decide. Shall we look at Hell first?"

"Sure!" said Bill. "Let's go!" Bill was amazed! He saw a clean, white sandy beach with clear waters. There were thousands of beautiful women running around, playing in the water, laughing and frolicking about. The sun was shining and the temperature was just perfect. Bill said: "This is great! If this is Hell, I can't wait to see Heaven!"

To which God replied: "Let's go!" and off they went. Bill saw puffy white clouds in a beautiful blue sky with angels drifting about playing harps and singing. It was nice, but surely not as enticing as Hell. Mr. Gates thought for only a brief moment and rendered his decision.

"God, I do believe I would like to go to Hell." "As you desire," said God.

Two weeks later, God decided to check up on the late billionaire to see how things were going. He found Bill shackled to a wall, screaming among the hot flames in a dark cave. He was being burned and tortured by demons.

"How ya doin, Bill?" asked God.

135

Bill responded with anguish and despair. "This is awful! This is not what I expected at all. What happened to the beach and the beautiful women playing in the water?"

"Oh, THAT!" said God. "That was the screen saver."

GRANDMA'S LETTER

The other day I went up to the local Christian bookstore and saw a honk if you love Jesus bumper sticker.

I was feeling particularly sassy that day because I had just come from a thrilling choir performance, followed by a thunderous prayer meeting, so I bought the sticker and put it on my bumper.

I was stopped at a red light at a busy intersection, just lost in thought about the Lord and how good He is and I didn't notice that the light had changed. It is a good thing someone else loves Jesus because if he hadn't honked, I'd never have noticed.

I found that LOTS of people love Jesus. Why, while I was sitting there the guy behind started honking like crazy, and when he leaned out of his window and screamed, "for the love of God, GO! GO!" What an exuberant cheerleader he was for Jesus.

Everyone started honking! I just leaned out of my window and started waving and smiling at all these loving people. I even honked my horn a few more times to share in the love. There must have been a man from Florida back there, because I heard him yelling something about a sunny beach...

I saw another guy waving in a funny way with only his middle finger stuck up in the air. When I asked my teenage grandson in the back seat what that meant, he said that it was probably a Hawaiian good luck sign or something. Well, I've never met anyone from Hawaii, so I leaned out the window and gave him a good luck sign back.

My grandson burst out laughing, why even he was enjoying this religious experience. A couple of the people were so caught up in the joy of the moment that they got out of their cars and started walking toward me. I bet they wanted to pray or ask what church I attended, but this is when I noticed the light had changed.

So, I waved to all my sisters and brothers grinning, and drove on through the intersection. I noticed I was the only car that got through the intersection before the light changed again and I felt kind of sad that I had to leave them after all the love we had shared, so I slowed the car down, leaned out of the window and gave them all the Hawaiian good luck sign one last time as I drove away.

Praise the Lord for such wonderful folks!

50 NATURAL HIGHS

1. Falling in love.
2. Laughing so hard your face hurts.
3. A hot shower.
4. No lines at the supermarket.
5. A special glance.
6. Getting mail.
7. Taking a drive on a pretty road.
8. Hearing your favorite song on the radio.
9. Lying in bed listening to the rain outside.
10. Hot towels fresh out of the dryer.
11. Finding the sweater you want is on sale for half price.
12. Chocolate milkshake. (or vanilla!) (or strawberry)
13. A long distance phone call.
14. A bubble bath.
15. Giggling.
16. A good conversation.
17. The beach.
18. Finding $5 in your coat pocket from last winter.
19. Laughing at yourself.
20. Midnight phone calls that last for hours.
21. Running through sprinklers.
22. Laughing for absolutely no reason at all.
23. Having someone tell you that you look good.
24. Laughing at an inside joke.
25. Friends.
26. Accidentally overhearing someone say something nice about you.

27. Waking up and realizing you still have a few hours left to sleep.

28. Your first kiss (either the very first or with a new partner).

29. Making new friends or spending time with old ones.

30. Playing with a new puppy.

31. Having someone play with your hair.

32. Sweet dreams.

33. Hot chocolate.

34. Road trips with friends.

35. Swinging on swings.

36. Wrapping presents under the Christmas tree while eating cookies and drinking your favorite beverage.

37. Song lyrics printed inside your new CD so you can sing along without feeling stupid.

38. Going to a really good concert.

39. Making eye contact with a cute stranger.

40. Winning a really competitive game.

41. Making chocolate ship cookies.

42. Having your friends send you homemade cookies.

43. Spending time with close friends.

44. Seeing smiles and hearing laughter from your friends.

45. Holding hands with someone you care about.

46. Running into an old friend and realizing that some things (good or bad) never change.

47. Riding the best roller coasters over and over.

48. Watching the expression on someone's face as they open a much desired present from you.

49. Watching the sunrise.

50. Getting out of bed every morning and being grateful for another beautiful day.

HOW MANY DOGS DOES IT TAKE TO CHANGE A LIGHT BULB?

Border Collie: Just one. And then I'll replace all the wiring that's no up to code.

Golden Retriever: The sun is shinning, the day is young, we've got our whole lives ahead of us, and you're inside worrying about a stupid light bulb?

Dachshund: You know I can't reach the stupid lamp.

Rottweiler: Make me.

Boxer: Who cares? I can still play with my squeaky toys in the dark.

Lab: Oh, Me, Me!!! Pleeeeeese let me change the light bulb! Can I? Can I? Huh? Huh? Can I? Pleeeeeeze, Please, Please?!?

German Shepard: I'll change it as soon as I've led these people from the dark, check to make sure I haven't missed any, and make one perimeter patrol to see that no one has tried to take advantage of the situation.

Jack Russell Terrier: I'll just pop it in while I am bouncing off the walls and the furniture.

Old English Sheep Dog: Light bulb? I'm sorry, I don't see a light bulb?

Cocker Spaniel: Why change it? I can still pee on the carpet in the dark.

Beagle: You talking to ME?

Chihuahua: Yo Quiero Taco Bulb?

Pointer: I see it, there it is, there it is, right there …

Greyhound: It isn't moving. Who cares?

Australian Shepard: First, I'll put all the light bulbs in a little circle ….

Poodle: I'll just blow in the Border Collie's ear, and he'll do it. By the time he finishes rewiring the house. My nails will be dry.

THE CAT: Dogs do not change light bulbs. People change light bulbs. So the real question is how long will it be before I can expect some light, some dinner, and a massage?

All of which proves, once again, that while dogs have masters, cats have staff.

RULES TO LIVE BY

Finally, the guy's side of the story. I must admit, it's pretty good. We always hear "the rules" from the female side. Now here are the rules from the male side. These are our rules!

(Please note … these are all numbered "1" on purpose!)

1. Learn to work the toilet seat. You're a big girl. If it's up, put it down. We need it up, you need it down. You don't hear us complaining about you leaving it down.
1. Sunday – Sports. It's like the full moon or a changing of the tides. Let it be.
1. Shopping is NOT a sport. And no, we are never going to think of it that way.
1 Crying is blackmail.
1. Ask for what you want. Let us be clear on this one: Subtle hints do not work! Strong hints do not work! Obvious hints do not work! Just say it!
1. Yes, and No are perfectly acceptable answers to almost every question.
1. Come to us with a problem only if you want help solving it. That's what we do. Sympathy is what your girlfriends are for.
1. A headache that lasts for 17 months is a problem. See a doctor.
1. Anything we said 6 months ago is inadmissible in an argument. In fact, all comments become null and void after 7 days.
1. If you won't dress like the Victoria's Secret girls, don't expect us to act like soap opera guys.
1. If you think you're fat, you probably are. Don't ask us.
1. If something we said can be interpreted two ways, and one of the ways makes you sad or angry, we meant the other one.
1. You can either ask us to do something or tell us how you want it done. Not both. If you already know best how to do it, just do it yourself.

1. Whenever possible, please say whatever you have to say during commercials.
1. Christopher Columbus did not need directions and neither do I.
1. ALL men see in only 16 colors, like windows default settings. Peach, for example, is a fruit, not a color. Pumpkin is also a fruit. We have no idea what mauve is.
1. If it itches, it will be scratched. We do that.
1. IF we ask what is wrong and you say "nothing," we will act like nothing is wrong. We know you are lying, but it is just not worth the hassle.
1. If you ask a question you don't want us to answer, expect an answer you don't want to hear.
1. When we have to go somewhere, absolutely anything you wear is fine … Really.
1. Don't ask us what we're thinking about unless you are prepared to discuss such topics as baseball, the shotgun formation, or monster trucks.
1. You have enough clothes.
1. You have too many shoes.
1. I am in shape. Round is a shape.
1. Thank you for reading this. Yes, I know, I have to sleep on the couch tonight, but did you know men really don't mind that, it's like camping.

Men who read this will laugh. Women will never understand it.

LISTEN

Little Johnny watched his daddy's car pass by the school playground and go into the woods. Curious, he followed the car and saw daddy and Aunt Jane in a passionate embrace. Little Johnny found this so exciting that he could not contain himself as he ran home and started to tell his mother.

"Mommy, I was at the playground and I saw daddy's car go into the woods with Aunt Jane. I went back to look and he was giving Aunt Jane a big kiss, then he helped her take off her shirt. Then Aunt Jane helped daddy take his pants off, then Aunt Jane ….."

At this point, mommy cut him off and said, "Johnny, this is such an interesting story, suppose you save the rest of it for supper time. I want to see the look on daddy's face when you tell it tonight."

At the dinner table, mommy asked little Johnny to tell his story. Johnny started his story about the car going into the woods, the undressing, Aunt Jane lying down on the back seat. Then Aunt Jane and daddy started doing the same thing that mommy and Uncle Bill used to do when daddy was in the Army.

Sometimes you need to listen to the whole story before you interrupt.

YOU KNOW YOU'RE FROM BOSTON IF...

1. You have to dial the area code to call your neighbor.
2. You think crosswalks are for babies.
3. Khaki's are something you start the car with.
4. You think if someone's nice to you, they either want something or they're from out of town (and possibly lost).
5. You know how to cross 4 lanes of traffic in 5 seconds.
6. If you hear someone say "pahk the cah in hahvad yahd" one more time you're going to bitch slap them upside the head.
7. Anything past Worcester is "the middle of nowhere".
8. You are amazed when traveling out of town that people who work at McDonald's speak English.
9. You think it's not actually tailgating unless your bumper is touching the car in front of you.
10. You know that a yellow light means at least 5 more cars can get through.
11. And that a red light means 2 more can.
12. Crown Victoria – undercover cop.
13. Subway is a fast food place. The transportation system is known as the "T", and only the "T".
14. For the cost of your house, you could own a small town in Iowa.
15. There are 6 Dunkin Donuts within 20 minutes of your house.
16. You or someone in your family has a Smart Tag.
17. When people talk about the "curse of the Bambino," you know what they're talking about (and believe in it too).
18. You know what the blinking red light atop of Hancock Tower means in the summer.
19. You think of Rhode Island as the "deep south."
20. You think the Yankees suck.

146

21. You believe using a turn signal "gives away your plan to the enemy."

22. If you stay on the same road long enough, it will eventually have 3 names.

23. Someone has honked at you because you didn't peel out the second the light turned green.

24. You've honked at someone because they didn't peel out the second the light turned green.

25. All potholes just add excitement to your driving experience.

26. Stop signs mean slow down a little, but only if you feel like it.

27. 6 inches of snow is considered a "dusting".

28. 3 days of 90+ heat is definitely a "heat wave" and 63 degree weather is "wicked warm."

29. $15 to park is a bargain.

30. You cringe every time you hear some actor/actress try to do "the Boston accent" in a movie – if you don't have it, you're never gonna get it right, even if you were born here.

31. The words wicked and mint once were major parts of your vocab, along with calling chocolate sprinkles at the ice cream shop "Jimmys"!

(NO TITLE)

A priest and a pastor from the local churches are standing by the side of the road, pounding a sign into the ground, which reads:

> The End is Near!
> Turn Yourself Around Now
> Before it's Too Late!

As a car sped past them, the driver yelled, "Leave us alone, you religious nuts!" From the curve they heard screeching tires and a big splash.

The pastor turns to the priest and asks, "Do you think the sign should just say 'Bridge Out'?"

HIGHER MATH

A professor of mathematics sent a fax to his wife. It read: "Dear Wife: You must realize that you are 54 years old, and I have certain needs which you are no longer able to satisfy. I am otherwise happy with you as wife, and I sincerely hope you will not be hurt or offended to learn that. By the time you receive this letter, I will be at the Grand Hotel with my 18-year old teaching assistant. I'll be home before midnight. Your Husband."

When he arrived at the hotel, there was a faxed letter waiting for him that read as follows:
"Dear Husband: You, too, are 54 years old, and by the time you receive this letter, I will be at Breakwater Hotel with the 18 year old pool boy. Being the brilliant mathematician that you are, you can easily appreciate the fact that 18 goes into 54 a lot more times than 54 goes into 18. Don't wait up."

AMEN

Heavenly Father, Help us remember that the jerk who cut us off in traffic last night is a single mother who worked nine hours that day and is rushing home to cook dinner, help with homework, do the laundry and spend a few precious moments with her children.
Help us to remember that the pierced, tattooed kid is an interesting young man who can't make change correctly and is a worried 19-year old college student, balancing his apprehension over final exams with his fear of not getting his student loans for next semester.

Remind us, Lord, that the scary looking bum, begging for money in the same spot every day (who really ought to get a job!) is a slave to addictions that we can only imagine in our worst nightmares.

Help us to remember that the old couple walking annoyingly slow through the store aisles and blocking our shopping progress are savoring this moment, knowing that, based on the biopsy report she got back last week, this will be the last year that they go shopping together.

Heavenly Father, remind us each day that, of all the gifts you give us, the greatest gift is love. It is not enough to share that love with those we hold dear. Open out hearts not to just those who are close to us, but to all humanity. Let us be slow to judge and quick to forgive, show patience, empathy and love. AMEN.

GOLFING TIPS

A friend just told me about a new instructional Golf Book by Bobby Rusher.

I haven't seen a copy yet; however, I did see a flyer, and from the list of chapters, it looks like it might be one in which you might have some interest. The title is:

"How to Line up Your 4th Putt", by Bobby Rusher

Here are some of the new book's more notable chapters:

A. How to hit a Top Flite from the rough when you hit a Titlist from the tee.

B. How to avoid the water when you lay 8 in the bunker.

C. How to get more distance out of a shank.

D. Using your shadow on the greens to maximize earnings.

E. Proper etiquette when you are playing with a complete jerk.

F. Crying and how to handle it.

G. How to rationalize a seven hour round.

H. How to find the ball that everyone else saw go into the water.

I. How to make hitting short of the ladies tee sexy.

J. How to let a 4-some play through your 2-some without getting embarrassed.

K. How to relax when you're hitting five off the tee.

L. When to suggest swing corrections to your opponent.

M. Honesty and the meaning of the double bogey.

Bobby is now working on the book's sequel, "When to Re-grip Your Ball Retriever."

IRISH DRIVER

Paddy the famous Irishman is driving home after downing a few at the local pub. He turns a corner and much to his horror he sees a tree in the middle of the road.

He swerves to avoid it and almost too late realizes that there is yet another tree directly in his path. He swerves again and discovers that his drive home has turned into a slalom course, causing him to veer from side to side to avoid all the trees.

Moments later he hears the sound of a police siren and brings his car to a stop. The officer approaches Paddy's car and asks him what on earth he was doing.

Paddy tells his story of the trees in the road when the officer stops him mid sentence and says, "Fer Chris sakes, Paddy, that's yer air freshener!"

THE LOVE DRESS

A woman stopped by unannounced at her recently married son's house. She rang the doorbell and walked in. She was shocked to see her daughter-in-law lying on the couch, totally naked. Soft music was playing and the aroma of perfume filled the room.

"What are you doing?" she asks.

"I'm waiting for my husband to come home from work," the daughter-in-law answered.

"But you're naked!" the mother-in-law exclaimed

"This is my LOVE dress," the daughter-in-law explained. "My husband LOVES me to wear this dress," she explained. "It excites him to no end. Every time he sees me in this dress, he instantly becomes romantic and ravages me for hours on end. He can't get enough of me."

The mother-in-law left. When she got home, she undressed, showered, put on her best perfume, dimmed the lights, put on a romantic CD, and lay on the couch waiting for her husband to arrive.

Finally, her husband came home. He walked in and saw her lying there so provocatively.

"What are you doing?" he asked.

"This is my LOVE dress," she whispered, sensually.

"Needs ironing," he said. "What's for dinner?"

CELEBRITY BRAIN CRAMPS

Q: If you could live forever, would you and why?
A: "I would not live forever, because we should not live forever, because if we were supposed to live forever, then we would live forever, but we cannot live forever, which is why I would not live forever."
---- Miss Alabama in the 1994 Miss USA Contest

"Whenever I watch TV and see those poor starving kids all over the world, I can't help but cry. I mean I'd love to be skinny that that, but not with all those flies and death and stuff."
---- Mariah Carey

"Smoking kills. If you're killed, you've lost a very important part of your life."
---- Brooke Shields, during an interview to become Spokesperson for federal anti-smoking campaign.

"I've never had major knee surgery on any other part of my body."
---- Winston Bennett, University of Kentucky basketball forward.

"Outside of the killings, Washington has one of the lowest crime rates in the country."
---- Mayor Marion Barry, Washington, DC

"I'm not going to have some reporters pawing through our papers. We are the president.
---- Hillary Clinton commenting on the release of the subpoenaed documents

"That lowdown scoundrel deserves to be kicked to death by a jackass, and I'm just the one to do it."
---- A congressional candidate in Texas

"It isn't pollution that's harming the environment; it's the impurities in our air and water that are doing it."

---- Al Gore, Vice President

"I love California. I practically grew up in Phoenix."
---- Dan Quayle

"It's no exaggeration to say that the undecideds could go one way or another."
---- George Bush, US President

"We've got to pause and ask ourselves: How much clean air do we need?"
---- Lee Iacocca

"I was provided with additional input that was radically different from the truth. I assisted in furthering that version."
---- Colonel Oliver North, from his Iran-Contra testimony

"The word 'genius' isn't applicable in football. A genius is a guy like Norman Einstein."
---- Joe Theisman, NFL football quarterback and sports analyst

"We don't necessarily discriminate. We simply exclude certain types of people."
---- Colonel Gerald Wellman, ROTC Instructor

"If we don't succeed, we run the risk of failure."
---- Bill Clinton, President

"We are ready for an unforeseen event that may or may not occur."
---- Al Gore, Vice President

"Traditionally, most of Australia's imports come from overseas."
---- Keppel Enderbery

"Your food stamps will be stopped effective March 1992, because we received notice that you passed away. May God bless you. You may reapply if there is a change in your circumstance."
---- Department of Social Service, Greenville, South Carolina

"If somebody has a bad heart, they can plug this jack in at night as they go to bed and it will monitor their heart throughout the night. And the next morning, when they wake up dead, there'll be a record."
---- Mark S. Fowler, FCC Chairman

SO YOU THINK YOU KNOW EVERYTHING

- A dime has 118 ridges around the edge.

- A cat has 32 muscles in each ear.

- A crocodile cannot stick out its tongue.

- A dragonfly has a life span of 24 hours.

- A goldfish has a memory span of three seconds.

- A "jiffy" is an actual unit of time for 1/100th of a second.

- A shark is the only fish that can blink with both eyes.

- A snail can sleep for three years.

- Al Capone's business card said he was a used furniture dealer.

- All 50 states are listed across the top of the Lincoln Memorial on the back of the $5 bill.

- Almonds are a member of the peach family.

- An ostrich's eye is bigger than its brain.

- Babies are born without kneecaps. They don't appear until the child reaches 2 to 6 years of age.

- Butterflies taste with their feet.

- Cats have over one hundred vocal sounds. Dogs only have about 10.

- "Dreamt" is the only English work that ends in the letters "mt".

- February 1865 is the only month in recorded history not to have a full moon.

- In the last 4,000 years, no new animals have been domesticated.

- If the population of China walked past you, in single file, the line would never end because of the rate of reproduction.

- If you are an average American, in your whole life, you will spend an average of six months waiting at red lights.

- It's impossible to sneeze with your eyes open.

- Leonardo Da Vinci invented scissors.

- Maine is the only state whose name is just one syllable.

- No word in the English language rhymes with month, orange, silver, or purple.

- On a Canadian two dollar bill, the flag flying over the Parliament building is an American flag.

- Our eyes are always the same size from birth, but our nose and ears never stop growing.

- Peanuts are one of the ingredients of dynamite.

- Rubber bands last longer when refrigerated.

- "Stewardesses" is the longest worded typed with only the left hand and "lollipop" with your right.

- The microwave was invented after a researcher walked by a radar tube and a chocolate bar melted in his pocket.

- The sentence: "the quick brown fox jumps over the lazy dog" uses every letter in the alphabet.

- The winter of 1932 was so cold that Niagara Falls froze completely solid.

- The words "racecar", "kayak", and "level" are the same whether they are read left to right or right to left (palindromes).

- There are 293 ways to make change for a dollar.

- There are more chickens than people in the world.

158

- There are only two words in the English language that have all five vowels in order: "abstemious" and "facetious".

- There's no Betty Rubble in the Flintstones Chewable Vitamins.

- Tigers have striped skin, not just striped fur.

- TYPEWRITER is the longest word that can be made using the letters on one row of the keyboard.

- Winston Churchill was born in a ladies' room during a dance.

- Your stomach has to produce a new layer of mucus every two weeks; otherwise it will digest itself.

- ………………………..Now you know everything!

THINGS I'VE LEARNED ABOUT FLORIDA

- Possums sleep in the middle of the road with their feet in the air.

- There are 5000 types of snakes, and 4998 live in Florida.

- There are 10,000 types of spiders. All 10,000 live in Florida, plus a couple that nobody has seen before.

- Squirrels will eat anything.

- Unknown critters love to dig holes under tomato plants.

- Raccoons will test your crop of melons and let you know when they are ripe.

- If it grows, it sticks; if it crawls, it bites.

- A tractor is NOT an all-terrain vehicle. They do get stuck.

- Onced and Twiced are words.

- It is not a shopping cart, it is a buggy.

- Fire ants consider your flesh as a picnic.

- People actually grow and eat okra.

- Fixinto is one word.

- There ain't no such thing as "lunch". There's dinner and there's "supper".

- Sweet tea is appropriate for all meals, and you start drinking it when you're two.

- Backwards and forwards means, "I know everything about you."

- Jeet? Is actually a phrase meaning "did you eat?"

- You don't have to wear a watch because it doesn't matter what time it is.

- You work until you're done or it's too dark to see.

- More about Florida …. You know you're from Florida if:
  - You measure distances in minutes.
  - You've ever had to switch from heat to air conditioning in the same day.
  - You see a car running in a store parking lot with no one in it no matter what time of the year.
  - You use "fix" as a verb. Example: I am fixinto go to the store.
  - All the festivals across the state are named after a fruit, vegetable, grain, insect or animal.
  - You install security lights on your house and garage and leave both unlocked.
  - You carry jumper cables in your car … for your own car.
  - You know what "cow tipping" is.
  - You only own four spices: salt, pepper, Texas Pete and catsup.
  - The local papers cover national and international news on one page and six pages for local gossip and sports.
  - You find 100 degrees Fahrenheit "a little warm".
  - You know all four seasons: almost summer, summer, still summer, and Christmas.
  - Going to Wal-Mart is a favorite past time known as "Goin' Wal-Martin" or "Off to 'Wally World'."
  - A carbonated soft drink isn't a soda, cola, or pop … it's a Coke, regardless of brand or flavor. Example: "What kina coke you want?"
  - Fried Catfish is the other white meat.
  - You understand these and forward them to your friends from Florida (and those who just wish they were).

ANDY ROONEY SAYS …
As I grow in age, I value women who are over 40 most of all. Here are just a few reasons why:

- An over 40 woman will never wake you in the middle of the night and ask, "What are you thinking?" She doesn't care what you think.

- If an over 40 woman doesn't want to watch the game, she doesn't sit around whining about it. She does something she wants to do. And it's usually something more interesting.

- An over 40 woman knows herself well enough to be assured in who she is, what she is, what she wants, and from whom. Few women past the age of 40 give a darn what you might think about her or what she's doing.

- An over 40 woman usually has had her fill of 'meaningful relationships' and "commitments." The last thing she wants in her life is another dopey, clingy, whiny, dependent lover.

- Over 40 women are dignified. They seldom have a screaming match with you at the opera or in an expensive restaurant. Of course, if you deserve it, they won't hesitate to shoot you if they think they can get away with it.

- Over 40 women are generous with praise, often undeserved. They know what it's like to be unappreciated.

- An over 40 woman has the self-assurance to introduce you to her women friends. A younger woman with a man will often ignore even her best friend because she doesn't trust the guy with other women. A woman over 40 couldn't care less if you're attracted to her friends because she knows her friends won't betray her.

- Women get psychic as they age. You never have to confess your sins to an over 40 woman. They always know.

- An over 40 woman looks good wearing bright red lipstick. This is not true of younger women.

- Over 40 women are forthright and honest. They'll tell you right off you are a jerk if you are acting like one. You don't ever have to wonder where you stand with her.

- Yes, we praise over 40 women for a multitude of reasons. Unfortunately, it's not reciprocal. For every stunning, smart, well-doffed hot woman of 40+, there is a bald, paunchy relic in yellow pants making a fool of himself with some 22-year-old waitress.

Ladies, I apologize.

THIS IS SUCH A NICE LETTER FROM THE PRESIDENT

The White House
Washington, DC
Mr. John Hinckley
St. Elizabeth's Hospital
Washington, DC

Dear John:

Laura and I hope that you are continuing your excellent progress in recovery from your mental problems. We are pleased to hear that you are now able to have unsupervised visits with your parents. The staff at the hospital report that you are doing fine.

I have decided to seek a second term in office as your President and would appreciate your support and the support of your fine parents.

I would hope that if there is anything that you need at the hospital, you would let us know.

By the way, are you aware that John Kerry is screwing Jody Foster?

Sincerely,

George W. Bush
President.

IRISH VIRGIN

In a tiny village on the Irish coast lived an old lady, a virgin and very proud of it.

Sensing that her final days were rapidly approaching, and desiring to make sure everything was in proper order when she dies, she went to the town's undertaker (who also happened to be the local postal clerk) to make the proper "final" arrangements.

As a last wish, she informed the undertaker that she wanted the following inscription engraved on her tombstone:
   "Born a Virgin, Lived as a Virgin, Died a Virgin"

Not long after, the old maid died peacefully, A few days after the funeral, as the undertaker - - postal clerk went to prepare the tombstone that the lady had requested, it became quite apparent that the tombstone that she had selected was much too small for the wording that she had chosen.

He thought long and hard about how he could fulfill the old maid's final request, considering the very limited space available on the small piece of stone.

For days, he agonized over the dilemma. But finally his experience as a postal worker allowed him to come up with what he thought was appropriate solution to the problem.

The virgin's tombstone was finally completed and duly engraved, and it reads as follows:

   "RETURNED UNOPENED"

LET IT BE

An Irishman in a wheelchair entered a restaurant one afternoon and asked the waitress for a cup of coffee. The Irishman looked across the restaurant and asked, "Is that Jesus sitting over there?"

The waitress nodded "yes," so the Irishman told her to give Jesus a cup of coffee on him.

The next patron to come in was an Englishman with a hunched back. He shuffled over to a booth, painfully sat down, and asked the waitress for a hot cup of tea. He also glanced across the restaurant and asked, "Is that Jesus over there?"

The waitress nodded, so the Englishman said to give Jesus a cup of hot tea, "My treat."

A third patron to come into the restaurant was a Redneck on crutches. He hobbled over to a booth, sat down and hollered, "Hey there, sweet thang. How's about getting me a cold glass of Coke." He, too, looked across the restaurant and asked, "Is that God's boy over there?"

The waitress once more nodded, so the Redneck said to give Jesus a cold glass of Coke, "On my bill."

As Jesus got up to leave, he passed by the Irishman, touched him and said, "For your kindness, you are healed." The Irishman felt the strength come back to his legs, got up, and danced a jig out the door.

Jesus also passed by the Englishman, touched him and said, "For your kindness, you are healed." The Englishman felt his back straightening up and he raised his hands, praised the Lord and did a series of back flips out the door.

Then Jesus walked towards the Redneck. The redneck jumped up and yelled, "Don't touch me ... I'm drawin' disability!"

SOMETIMES

- Sometimes ... when you cry, no one sees your tears.
- Sometimes ... when you are in pain, no one sees your hurt.
- Sometimes ... when you are worried, no one sees your stress.
- Sometimes ... when you are happy, no one sees your smile.
- But fart just one time!...

READING TEST

I cdnuolt blveiee taht I cluod aulaclty uesdnatnud what I wss rdgnieg.

The paomnnehal pweor of the hmuan mnid.

According to a rscheearch at Cmabrigde Uinervtisy, it deosn't mttaer in waht oredr the ltteers in a wrod are, the olny iprmoatnt tihng is taht the frist and lsat ltteer be in the rghit pclae. The rset can be a taotl mses and you can sitll raed it wouthit porbelm. Tihs is bcuseae the huamn mnid deos not raed ervey lteter by istlef, but the wrod as a wlohe.

Amzanig huh?

WHAT RELIGION IS YOUR BRA

A man walked into the ladies department of a Macy's and shyly walked up to the woman behind the counter and said "I'd like to buy a bra for my wife."

"What type of bra" asked the clerk?

"Type?" inquires the man. "There's more than one type?"

"Look around," said the saleslady, as she showed a sea of bras in every shape, size, color and material imaginable.

"Actually, even with all of this variety, there are really only four types of bras to choose from."

Relieved, the man asked about the types.

The saleslady replied, "There are the Catholic, the Salvation Army, the Presbyterian, and the Baptist types. Which one would you prefer?"

Now totally befuddled, the man asked about the difference between them.

The saleslady responded, "It is all really quite simple ... the Catholic type supports the masses, the Salvation Army type lifts the fallen, the Presbyterian type keeps them staunch and upright, and the Baptist makes mountains out of mole hills."

Bra sizes: Have you ever wondered why A, B, C, D, DD, E, F, G and H are the letters used to define bra sizes? If you have wondered why, but couldn't figure out what the letters stood for, it is about time you became informed!

      (A)   Almost Boobs ...

(B)   Barely there.
(C)   Can't Complain!
(D)   Dang!
(DD) Double Dang!
(E)   Enormous!
(F)   Fake.
(G)   Get a Reduction.
(H)   Help me, I've fallen and I can't get up!

SILENT TREATMENT

Mike and Joan were having some problems at home and were giving each other the "silent treatment." But then Mike realized that he would need his wife to wake him at 5:00 am for an early morning drive with some pals to a golf match. Not wanting to be the first to break the silence (and so lose the "war"), he wrote on a piece of paper, "Please wake me at 5:00 am."

The next morning, Mike woke up, only to discover it was 9:00 am and his friends would have left for the golf course without him. Furious, he was about to go and see why his wife hadn't awakened him when he noticed a piece of paper by the bed. The paper said, "It is 5:00 am. Wake up."

Men simply are not equipped for these kinds of contests.

A DINNER CONVERSATION THAT WENT WRONG

Wife: "What would you do if I died? Would you get married again?"
Husband: "Definitely not!"
Wife: "Why not – don't you like being married?"
Husband: "Of course I do."
Wife: "then why wouldn't you remarry?"
Husband: "Okay, I'd get married again."
Wife: "You would? (with a hurtful look on her face)."
Husband: (makes audible groan).
Wife: "Would you sleep with her in our bed?"
Husband: "Where else would we sleep?"
Wife: "Would you replace my pictures with hers?"
Husband: "That would seem like the proper thing to do."
Wife: "Would she use my golf clubs?"
Husband: "No, she's left-handed."
Wife: ...... silence ......
Husband: "Shit."

FISHING STORY

Once upon a time, long, long ago there was a Presidential election that was too close to call. Neither the Republican presidential candidate nor the Democratic presidential candidate had enough votes to win the election.

Therefore, it was decided that there should be an ice fishing contest between the two candidates to determine the final winner. There was much talk about ballot recounting, court challenges, etc., but a week-long ice fishing competition seemed the (manly) way to settle things. The candidate that catches the most fish at the end of the week wins.

After a lot of back and forth discussion, it was decided that the contest would take place on a remote and cold lake in Wisconsin. There were to be no observers present, and both men were to be sent out separately on this remote lake and return daily with their catch for counting and verification.

At the end of the first day, Kerry returns to the starting line and he has 10 fish. Soon, W. returns and has zero fish. Well, everyone assumes he is just having another bad day or something and hopefully, he will catch up the next day. At the end of the second day Kerry comes in with 20 fish and W. comes in again with none.

That evening, Dick Chaney gets together secretly with W. and says, "I think Kerry is a lowlife cheatin' son-of-a-gun. I want you to go out tomorrow and don't even bother with fishing. Just spy on him and see if he is cheating in any way.

The next night (after Kerry comes back with 50 fish), Cheney says to Bush, "Well, what about it, is Kerry cheatin'?" "He sure is, Dick, he's cutting holes in the ice."

TAMPA BAY LIGHTENING FANS

On a tour of Florida, the Pope took a couple of days off to visit the west coast for some sightseeing. He was cruising along the beach in the Pope mobile when there was a frantic commotion just off shore. A helpless man, wearing a Calgary Flames jersey, was struggling frantically to free himself from the jaws of a 25-foot shark.

As the Pope watched, horrified, a speedboat came racing up with three men wearing Tampa Bay Lightning jerseys aboard.

One quickly fired a harpoon into the shark's side. The other two reached out and pulled the pleading, semiconscious Flames fan from the water.

Then using baseball bats, the three heroes in Lightning garb beat the shark to death and hoisted it into the boat.

Immediately the Pope shouted and summoned them to the beach. "I give you my blessing for your brave actions," he told them. "I heard that there was some bitter hatred between Lightning and Flames fans, but now I have seen with my own eyes that this is not the truth."

As the Pope drove off, the harpooner asked his buddies, "Who was that?"

"It was the Pope," one replied. "He is in direct contact with God and has access to all of God's wisdom."

"Well," the harpooner said, "he may have God's wisdom, but he doesn't know shit about shark fishing ... how's the bait holding up?"

WEIRD HISTORY

Have a history teacher explain this … if they can!
Abraham Lincoln was elected to congress in 1846.
John F. Kennedy was elected to Congress in 1946.

Abraham Lincoln was elected President in 1860.
John F. Kennedy was elected President in 1960.

Both were particularly concerned with civil rights.
Both wives lost their husbands while living in the White House.
Both presidents were shot on a Friday.
Both presidents were shot in the head.

Now this is really weird:
Lincoln's secretary was named Kennedy.
Kennedy's secretary was named Lincoln.

Both were assassinated by southerners.
Both were succeeded by southerners named Johnson.
Andrew Johnson, who succeeded Lincoln, was born in 1808.
Lyndon Johnson, who succeeded Kennedy, was born in 1908.
John Wilkes Booth, who assassinated Lincoln, was born in 1839.
Lee Harvey Oswald, who assassinated Kennedy, was born in 1939.
Both assassins were known by their three names.
Both names are composed of fifteen letters.

Now hang on to your seat.
Lincoln was shot in a theatre named "Ford".
Kennedy was shot in a car called "Lincoln" made by "Ford".
Lincoln was shot in a theatre and his assassin ran and hid in a warehouse.
Kennedy was shot from a warehouse and his assassin ran and hid in a theatre.
Booth and Oswald were assassinated before their trials.

And here's the kick … A week before Lincoln was shot, he was in Monroe, Maryland.
A week before Kennedy was shot, he was with Marilyn Monroe.

NEW EDITION OF "YOU KNOW YOU'RE A REDNECK WHEN ..."

1. You take your dog for a walk and you both use the same tree.
2. You can entertain yourself for more than 15 minutes with a fly swatter.
3. Your boat has not left the driveway in 15 years.
4. You burn your yard rather than mow it.
5. You think the "Nutcracker" is something you do off the high dive.
6. The Salvation Army declines for furniture.
7. You offer to give someone the shirt off your back and they don't want it.
8. You have the local taxidermist on speed dial.
9. You come back from the dump with more than you took.
10. You keep a can of Raid on the kitchen table.
11. Your wife can climb a tree faster than your cat.
12. Your grandmother has "ammo" on her Christmas list.
13. You keep flea and tick soap in the shower.
14. You've been involved in a custody fight over a hunting dog.
15. You go to the stock car races and don't need a program.
16. You know how many bales of hay your car will hold.
17. You have a rag for a gas cap.
18. Your house doesn't have curtains, but your truck does.
19. You wonder how service stations keep their restrooms so clean.
20. You can spit without opening your mouth.
21. You consider your license plate personalized because your father made it.
22. Your lifetime goal is to own a fireworks stand.

23. You have a complete set of salad bowls and they all say "Cool Whip" on the side.

24. The biggest city you've ever been to is Wal-Mart.

25. Your working TV sits on top of your non-working TV.

26. You've used your ironing board as a buffet table.

27. A tornado hits your neighborhood and does a $100,000 worth of improvements.

28. You've used a toilet brush to scratch your back.

29. You missed your 5th grade graduation because you were on jury duty.

30. You think fast food is hitting a deer at 65 mph.

31. Somebody tells you that you've got something in your teeth, so you take them out to see what it is!

BLOND JOKE

A blind man walks into a bar. He finds his way to a bar stool and orders a drink. After sitting there for a while, he yells to the bartender in a loud voice, "Hey bartender, you wanna hear a dumb blond joke?" The bar immediately falls deathly quiet.

In a very deep, husky voice, the woman next to him says, "before you tell that joke, sir, I think it is just fair, given that you are blind, that you should know five things:

1. The bartender is a blond woman.
2. The bouncer is a blond woman.
3. The woman sitting next to me is blond and is a professional weightlifter.
4. The lady to your right is a blond and is a professional wrestler, and
5. I'm a 6 foot, 200 lb. blond woman with a PhD., a black belt in karate and a very bad attitude!

Now think about it seriously, Mister. Do you still want to tell that joke?"

The blind man thinks for a second, shakes his head, and says, "Nah … not if I'm gonna have to explain it five times."

YOU CAN TAKE IT WITH YOU

There was a man who had worked all of his life, had saved all of his money, and was a real miser when it came to his money. Just before he died, he said to his wife, "When I die, I want you to take all my money and put it in the casket with me. I want to take my money to the afterlife with me."

And so he got his wife to promise him with all of her heart that when he died, she would put all of the money in the casket with him. Well, he died. He was stretched out in the casket, his wife was sitting there in black, and her friend was sitting next to her. When they finished the ceremony, just before the undertakers got ready to close the casket, the wife said, "Wait just a minute!" She had a box with her; she came over with the box and put it in the casket. Then the undertakers locked the casket down, and they rolled it away.

So her friend said, "Girl, I know you weren't fool enough to put all that money in there with your husband."

The loyal wife replied, "Listen, I'm a Christian, I can't go back on m word. I promised him that I was going to put that money in the casket with him."

"You mean to tell me you put that money in the casket with him !!!?"

"I sure did," said the wife. "I got it all together, put it into my account and wrote him a check. If he can cash it, he can spend it."

NUDIST COLONY

A man joins a very exclusive nudist colony. On his first day there he takes off his clothes and starts to wander around. A gorgeous petite blonde walks by, and the man immediately gets an erection. The woman notices his erection, comes over to him and says, "Did you call for me?"

The man replies "No; what do you mean?"

She says, "You must be new here. Let me explain. It's a rule here that if you get an erection it implies you called for me." Smiling, she leads him to the side of the swimming pool, lies down on a towel, eagerly pulls him to her and happily lets him have his way with her.

The man continues to explore the colony's facilities. He enters the sauna and as he sits down, he farts. Within minutes a huge, hairy man lumbers out of the steam room toward him, "Did you call for me?" says the hairy man.

"No, what do you mean?" says the newcomer.

"You must be new," says the hairy man, "it's a rule that if you fart, it implies that you called for me." The huge man easily spins him around, bends him over a bench and has his way with him.

The newcomer staggers back to the colony office, where he is greeted by the smiling, naked receptionist, "May I help you?" she says. The man yells "Here's my membership card. You can have the key back and you can keep the $500 membership fee."

"But sir," she replies, "you've only been here for a few hours. You haven't had the chance to see all our facilities."

The man replies, "Listen lady, I'm 68 years old; I only get an erection once a month, I fart 15 times a day; I'm outta here!"

LETTERS TO GOD FROM DOGS

Dear God:

Why do humans smell the flowers, but seldom, if ever, smell one another?

When we get to heaven, can we sit on your couch? Or is it the same old story?

Why are there cars named after the jaguar, the cougar, the mustang, the colt, the stingray, and the rabbit, but no ONE named for a dog? How often do you see a cougar riding around? We dogs love a nice ride!

Would it be so hard to rename the 'Chrysler Eagle' the 'Chrysler Beagle'?

If a dog barks his head off in the forest and no human hears him, it he still a bad dog?

We dogs can understand human verbal instructions, hand signals, whistles, horns, clickers, beepers, scent ID's, electromagnetic energy fields, and Frisbee flight paths. What do humans understand?

More meatballs, less spaghetti, please!

When we get to the Pearly Gates, do we have to shake hands to get in?

Are there mailmen in Heaven? If there are, will I have to apologize?

Let me give you a list of just some of the things I must remember to be a good dog:

- I will not eat the cats' food before they eat it or after they throw it up.

- I will not roll on dead seagulls, fish, crabs, etc., just because I like the way they smell.

- The sofa is not a face towel; neither are Mom and Dad's laps.

- The garbage collector is not stealing our stuff.

- My head does not belong in the refrigerator.

- I will not bite the officer's hand when he reaches in for Mon's driver's license and registration.

- I will not play tug-of-war with Dad's underwear when he's on the toilet.

- Sticking my nose into someone's crotch is not an acceptable way of saying 'hello'.

- I do not need to suddenly stand straight up when I'm lying under the coffee table.

- I must shake the rainwater out of my fur before entering the house.

- I will not throw up in the car.

- I will not come in from outside and immediately drag my butt across the carpet.

- I will not sit in the middle of the living room and lick my crotch when company is over.

- The cat is not a squeaky toy; so when I play with him and he makes that noise, it's usually not a good thing.

And Dear God, may I have my testicles back?

WOMEN'S ASS SIZE STUDY

There is a new study out about women and how they feel about their asses!

I thought the results were pretty interesting:

- 85% of women think their ass is too big ...
- 10% of women think their ass is too little ....
- The other 5% say that they don't care, they love him, he's a good man, and they would have married him anyway.

DYSFUNCTIONAL SECTION OF A HALLMARK STORE

1. I always wanted to have someone to hold, someone to love. And now that you've come into my life ... (inside card) - I've changed my mind.

2. I must admit, you brought religion into my life ... (inside card - I never believed in Hell until I met you.

3. As the days go by, I think how lucky I am ... (inside card) - That you're not here to ruin it for me.

4. Congratulations on your promotion. Before you go ... (inside card) - Will you take the knife from my back? You'll probably need it again.

5. Someday I hope to marry ... (inside card) - Someone other than you.

6. Happy Birthday! You look great for your age ... (inside card) - Almost lifelike!

7. When we were together, you said you'd die for me ... (inside card) - Now we've broken up, I think it's time to keep your promise.

8. We've been friends for a very long time ... (inside card) - What do you say we stop?

9. I'm so miserable without you ... (inside card) - It's almost like you're still here.

10. Congratulations on your new bundle of joy ... (inside card) - Did you ever find out who the father was?

11. You are such a good friend. If we were on a sinking ship and there was only one life jacket ... (inside card) - I'd miss you terribly and think of you often.

12. Your friends and I wanted to do something special for your Birthday ... (inside card) - So we're having you put to sleep.

13. Happy Birthday, Uncle Dad! ... (inside card) - Available only in Alabama, Mississippi, Arkansas and Kentucky.

14. Looking back over the years we've been together, I can't help but wonder ... (inside card) - What was I thinking?

15. Congratulations on your wedding day! ... (inside card) - Too bad no one likes your husband.

GREAT OLYMPIC MOMENTS

Here are the top nine comments made by NBC commentators during the Summer Olympics that they would like to take back:

1. Weightlifting commentator: "This is Gregoriava from Bulgaria. I saw her snatch this morning during her warm up and it was amazing."
2. Dressage commentator: "This is really a lovely horse and I speak from personal experience since I once mounted her mother.
3. Paul Hamm, Gymnast: "I owe a lot to my parents, especially my mother and father."
4. Boxing Analyst: "Sure there have been injuries, and even some deaths boxing, but none of them really that serious."
5. Softball announcer: "If history repeats itself, I should think we can expect the same thing again."
6. Basketball analyst: "He dribbles a lot and the opposition doesn't like it. In fact, you can see it all over their faces."
7. At the rowing medal ceremony: "Ah, isn't that nice, the wife of the IOC President is hugging the cox of the British crew."
8. Soccer commentator: "Julian Dicks is everywhere. It's like they've got eleven Dicks on the field."
9. Tennis commentator: "One of the reasons Andy is playing so well is that, before the final round, his wife takes out his balls and kisses them ... my God, what have I just said?"

WHO SAYS COPS DON'T HAVE A SENSE OF HUMOR?

"Relax, the handcuffs are tight because they're new. They'll stretch out after you wear them awhile."

"Take you hands off the car and I'll make your birth certificate a worthless document."

"If you run, you'll only go to jail tired."

"Can you run faster than 1,200 feet per second? In case you didn't know, that is the speed of a 9 mm bullet fired from my gun."

"So you don't know how fast you were going. I guess that means I can write anything I want on the ticket, huh?"

"Yes, sir, you can talk to the shift supervisor, but I don't think it will help. Oh … did I mention that I am the shift supervisor?"

"Warning! You want a warning? O.K., I'm warning you not to do that again or I'll give you another ticket."

"The answer to this last question will determine whether you are drunk or not. Was Mickey Mouse a cat or a dog?"

"Fair? You want me to be fair? Listen, fair is a place where you go to ride on rides, eat cotton candy, and step in monkey poop."

"Yeah, we have a quota. Two more tickets and my wife gets a toaster oven."

"In God we trust, all others we run through NCIC."

"No, sir, we don't have quotas anymore. We used to have quotas but now we're allowed to write as many tickets as we want."

"I'm glad to hear the Chief of Police is a good personal friend of yours. At least you know someone who can post your bail."

"You didn't think we gave pretty women tickets? You're right, we don't. Sign here."

30 YEARS, WHAT A DIFFERENCE

1974: Long hair ... 2004: Longing for hair.
1974: The perfect high ... 2004: The perfect high yield mutual fund.
1974: KEG ... 2004: EKG
1974: Acid rock ... 2004: Acid reflux.
1974: Moving to California because it's cool ... 2004: Moving to California because it's warm.
1974: Growing pot ... 2004: Growing pot belly.
1974: Trying to look like Marlon Brando or Liz Taylor ... 2004: Trying not to look like Marlon Brando or Liz Taylor.
1974: Seeds and stems ... 2004: Roughage.
1974: Killer weed ... 2004: Weed killer.
1974: Hoping for a BMW ... 2004 Hoping for a BM.
1974: The Grateful Dead ... 2004: Dr. Kevorkian.
1974: Going to a new, hip joint ... 2004: Receiving a new hip joint.
1974: Rolling Stones ... 2004: Kidney Stones.
1974: Screw the system ... 2004: Upgrade the system.
1974: Disco ... 2004: Costco.
1994: Passing the driver's test ... 2004: Passing the vision test.
1974: Whatever ... 2004: Depends.

Just in case you weren't feeling old today, this will certainly change things. Each year the staff at Beloit College in Wisconsin puts together a list to try to give the faculty a sense of the mindset of this year's incoming freshman. Here's this years list (2004):

- The people who are starting college this fall across the nation were born in 1985. They are too young to remember the space shuttle blowing up.

- Their lifetime has always included AIDS.

- Bottle caps have always been screw off and plastic.

- The CD was introduced the year they were born.

- They have always had an answering machine.

- They have always had cable.

- They cannot fathom not having a remote control.

- Jay Leno has always been on the Tonight Show.

- Popcorn has always been cooked in the microwave.

- They never took a swim and thought about Jaws.

- They can't imagine what hard contact lenses are.

- They don't know who Mork was or where he was from.

- They never heard: "Where's the Beef?" "I'd walk a mile for a Camel, or "de plane Boss, de plane."

- They do not care who shot J.R. and have no idea who J.R. even is.

- They don't have a clue how to use a typewriter.

Do you feel old now? Nah…

YOU MIGHT BE A FLORIDIAN IF:
(This comes after the 2004 Hurricane Season)

- You exhibit a slight twitch when introduced to anyone with the first name of Charley, Frances or Ivan.

- Your freezer never has more than $20 worth of food in it any given time.

- You're looking at paint swatches for the plywood on you windows, to accent the house color.

- You think of your hall closet/saferoom as "cozy".

- Your pool is more accurately described as "framed in" than "screened in".

- Your freezer in the garage now only has homemade ice in it.

- You no longer worry about relatives visiting during the summer months.

- You too haven't heard back from the insurance adjuster.

- You now understand what that little "2% hurricane deductible" phrase really means.

- You're putting a collage together on your driveway of roof shingles from your neighborhood.

- You were once proud of your 16" electric chain saw.

- Your Street has more than 3 "No Wake" signs posted.

- You own 5 large ice chests.

- Your parrot can now say "hammered, pounded and hunker down".

- You recognize people in line at the free ice, gas and plywood locations.

- You stop what you're doing and clap and wave when you see a convoy of power trucks come down your street.

- You're depressed when they don't stop.

- You have the personal cell phone numbers of the managers for: plywood, roofing supplies and generators at home Depot on your speed dial.

- You've spent more than $20 on "Tall white kitchen bags" to make your own sand bags.

- You're considering upgrading your 16" to a 20" chainsaw.

- You know what "Bar chain oil" is.

- You now think the $6000 whole house generator seems reasonable.

- You look forward to discussions about the merits of "cubed, block and dry ice".

- Your therapist refers to your condition as "generator envy".

- You fight the urge to put on your winter coat and wool cap and parade around in front your picture window, when you finally get power and your neighbor across the street, with the noisy generator doesn't get electric.

- And finally, you might be a Floridian if - You ask your sister up north to start saving the Sunday Real Estate Classifieds!

GETTING READY FOR HURRICANE SEASON

We're about to enter the peak of the hurricane season. Any day now, you're going to turn on the TV and see a weather person pointing to some radar blob out in the Atlantic Ocean and making tow basic meteorological points:
1. There is no need to panic.
2. We could all be killed.

Yes, hurricane season is an exciting time to be in Florida. If you're new to the area, you're probably wondering what you need to do to prepare for the possibility that we'll get hit by "the big one." Based on our experiences, we recommend that you follow this simple three-steep preparedness plan:
1. Buy enough food and bottled water to last your family for at least three days.
2. Put these supplies into your car.
3. Drive to Iowa and remain there until Halloween.

Unfortunately, statistics show that most people will not follow this sensible plan. Most people will foolishly stay in Florida.

We'll start with one of the most important hurricane preparedness items:

HOMEOWNERS' INSURANCE:
If you own a home, you must have hurricane insurance. Fortunately, this insurance is cheap and each to get, as long as your home meets two basic requirements:
1. It is reasonably well-built, and
2. It is located in Iowa.

Unfortunately, if your home is located in Florida, or any other area that might actually be hit by a hurricane, most insurance companies would prefer not to sell you hurricane insurance, because then they might be required to pay YOU money, and that is certainly not why they got into the insurance business in the first place. So you'll have to scrounge around for an insurance company, which will charge you an annual premium roughly equal to the replacement value of your house. At any moment, this company can drop you like used dental floss. Since Hurricane George, I have had an estimated 27 different home-insurance companies. This week, I'm covered by the Bob and Big Stan Insurance Company, under a policy which states that, in addition to my premium, Bob and Big Stan are entitled, on demand, to my kidneys.

SHUTTERS:
Your house should have hurricane shutters on all the windows, all the doors, and—if it's a major hurricane—all the toilets. There are several types of shutters, with advantages and disadvantages:
Plywood shutters: The advantage is that, because you make them yourself, they're cheap. The disadvantage is that, because you make them yourself, they will fall off.
Sheet-metal shutters: The advantage is that these work well, once you got them all up. The disadvantage is that once you get them all up, your hands will be useless bleeding stumps, and it will be December.
Roll-down shutters: The advantages are that they're very easy to use, and will definitely protect your house. The disadvantage is that you will have to sell your house to pay for them.

Hurricane-proof windows: These are the newest wrinkle in hurricane protection: They look like ordinary windows, but they can withstand hurricane winds! You can be sure of this, because the salesman says so. He lives in Iowa.

Hurricane Proofing your property: As the hurricane approaches, check your yard for movable objects like barbecue grills, planters, patio furniture, visiting relatives, etc … You should, as a precaution, throw these items into your swimming pool (if you don't have a swimming pool, you should have one built immediately). Otherwise, the hurricane winds will turn these objects into deadly missiles.

EVACUATION ROUTE:
If you live in a low-lying area, you should have an evacuation route planned out. (To determine whether you live in a low-lying area, look at your driver's license; if it says "Florida," you live in a low-lying

area). The purpose of having an evacuation route is to avoid being trapped in your home when a major storm hits. Instead, you will be trapped in a gigantic traffic jam several miles from your home, along with two hundred thousand other evacuees. So, as a bonus, you will not be lonely.

HURRICANE SUPPLIES:
If you don't evacuate, you will need a mess of supplies. Do not buy them now! Florida tradition requires that you wait until the last possible minute, then go to the supermarket and get into vicious fights with strangers over who gets the last can of SPAM. In addition to food and water, you will need the following supplies:

1. 23 Flashlights. At least $167 worth of batteries that turn out, when the power goes off, to be the wrong size for the flashlights.

2. Bleach. (No, I don't know what the bleach is for. NOBODY knows what the bleach is for, but it's traditional. So get some!)

3. 55 gallon drum of underarm deodorant.

4. A big knife that you can strap to your leg. (This will be useless in a hurricane, but it looks cool.)

5. A large quantity of raw chicken, to placate the alligators. (Ask anybody who went through Andrew; after the hurricane, there WILL be irate alligators.)

6. $35,000 in cash or diamonds so that, after hurricane draws passes, you can buy a generator from a man with no discernible teeth.

Of course these are just basic precautions. As the hurricane draws near, it is vitally important that you keep abreast of the situation by turning on your television and watching TV reporters in rain slickers stand right next to the ocean and tell you over and over how vitally important it is for everybody to stay away from the ocean.

Good luck, and remember: It's great living in Paradise.

TRANSATLANTIC FLIGHT

On a transatlantic flight, a plane passes through a severe storm. The turbulence is awful, and things go from bad to worse when one wing is struck by lightning. One woman in particular loses it. Screaming, she stands up in the front of the plane. "I'm too young to die" she wails. Then she yells, "Well, if I'm going to die, I want my last minutes on earth to be memorable! Is there someone on this plane who can make me feel like a WOMAN?"

For a moment there is silence. Everyone has forgotten their own peril. They all stare. Eyes riveted, at the desperate woman in the front of the plane. Then a man from Texas stands up in the rear of the plane. He is handsome: tall, well built, with dark brown hair and hazel eyes. He starts to walk slowly up the aisle, unbuttoning his shirt, slowly – one button at a time. No one move. He removes his shirt. Muscles ripple across his chest. She gasps …

He says, "Iron this – and then get me a beer."

DO YOU REMEMBER WHEN?...

- All the girls had ugly gym uniforms?

- It took five minutes for the TV to warm up?

- Nearly everyone's mom was at home when the kids got home from school?

- Nobody owned a purebred dog?

- When a quarter was a decent allowance?

- You'd reach into a muddy gutter for a penny?

- Your mom wore nylons that came in two pieces?

- All your male teachers wore neckties and female teachers had their hair done every day and wore high heels?

- You got your windshield cleaned, oil checked, and gas pumped, without asking, all for free, every time?

- And you didn't pay for air? And you got trading stamps to boot?

- Laundry detergent has free glasses, dishes or towels hidden inside the box?

- It was considered a great privilege to be taken out to dinner at a real restaurant with your parents?

- They threatened to keep kids back a grade if they failed .. and they did?

- When a 57 Chevy was everyone's dream car ... to cruise, peel out, lay rubber or watch submarine races, and people went steady?

- No one ever asked where the car keys were because they were always in the car, in the ignition, and the doors were never locked?

- Lying on your back in the grass with your friends and saying things like, "That cloud look like a …"

- And playing baseball with no adults to help kids with the rules of the game?

- Stuff from the store came without safety saps and hermetic seals because no one had yet tried to poison a perfect stranger?

- And with all our progress, don't you just wish, just once, you could slip back in time and savor the slower pace, and share it with the children of today?

- When being sent to the principal's office was nothing compared to the fate that awaited the student at home? Basically we were in fear for out lives, but it wasn't because of drive-by shootings, drugs, gangs, etc.

- Our parents and grandparents were a much bigger threat! But we survived because their love was greater than the threat.

- Send this a on to someone who can still remember Nancy Drew, the Hardy Boys, Laurel and Hardy, Howdy Dowdy and the Peanut Gallery, the Lone Ranger, The Shadow Knows, Nellie Bell, Roy and Dale, Trigger and Buttermilk.

- As well as summers filled with bike rides, baseball games, Hula Hoops, bowling and visits to the pool, and eating Kool-Aid powder with sugar.

Didn't that feel good, just to go back and say, "Yea, I remember that"? I am sharing this with you today because it ended with a double dare to pass it on. To remember that the perfect age is somewhere between old enough to know better and too young to care.

HOW MANY OF THESE DO YOU REMEMBER?

- Candy cigarettes.
- Wax Coke-shaped bottles with colored sugar water inside.
- Soda pop machines that dispensed glass bottles.
- Coffee shops with tableside jukeboxes.
- Blackjack, Clove and Teaberry chewing gum.
- Home milk delivery in glass bottles with cardboard stoppers.
- Newsreels before the movie.
- P.F. Fliers.
- Telephone numbers with a word prefix ... (Grandview 4-6801)
- Peashooters.
- Howdy Dowdy.
- 45 RPM records.
- Green Stamps.
- Hi-Fi's.
- Metal ice cube trays with levers.
- Mimeograph paper.
- Beanie and Cecil.
- Roller-skate keys.
- Cork pop guns.
- Drive Ins.
- Studebakers.
- Wash tub wringers.

- The Fuller Brush Man.
- Reel-to-Reel tape recorders.
- Tinker toys.
- Erector Sets.
- The Fort Apache Play Set.
- Lincoln Logs.
- 15 cent McDonald hamburgers.
- 5 cent packs of baseball cards – with that awful pink slab of bubble gum.
- Penny candy.
- 35 cents a gallon gasoline.
- Jiffy Pop popcorn.

DO YOU REMEMBER A TIME WHEN ...

- Decisions were made by going "eeny-meeny-miney-moe"?

- Mistakes were corrected by simply exclaiming, "Do Over!"?

- "Race issues" meant arguing about who ran the fastest?

- Catching the fireflies could happily occupy an entire evening?

- It wasn't odd to have two or three "Best Friends"?

- The worst thing you could catch from the opposite sex was "cooties"?

- Having a weapon in school meant being caught with a slingshot?

- A foot of snow was a dream come true?

- Saturday morning cartoons weren't 30-minute commercials for actions figures?

- "Oly-oly-oxen-free" made perfect sense?

- Spinning around, getting dizzy, and falling down was cause for giggles?

- The worst embarrassment was being picked last for a team?

- War was a card game?

- Baseball cards in the spokes transformed any bike into a motorcycle?

- Taking drugs meant orange-flavored chewable aspirin?

- Water balloons were the ultimate weapon?

If you can remember most or all of these, then you have lived !!!!!

Pass this on to anyone who may need a break from their "grown-up" life … I double-dog-dare-ya!

NOT A GOOD COMPARISON

A man and his wife were working in their garden one day and the man looks over at his wife and says: "Your butt is getting really big, I mean really big. I bet your butt is bigger that the barbecue." With that he proceeded to get a measuring tape and measured the grill and then went over to where his wife was working and measured his wife's bottom.

"Yes, I was right, your butt is two inches wider than the barbecue!!!" The woman chose to ignore her husband. Later that night in bed, the husband is feeling a little frisky. He makes some advances towards his wife who completely brushes him off.

"What's wrong?" he asks.

She answers: "Do you really think I'm going to fire up this big-ass grill for one little weenie?"

JESUS COULD HAVE BEEN....

There are 3 good arguments that Jesus could have been black:
1. He called everyone "brother".
2. He liked Gospel!
3. He couldn't get a fair trial.

But then there were 3 equally good arguments that Jesus was Jewish:
1. He went into His Father's business.
2. He lived at home until he was 33.
3. He was sure his Mother was a virgin and his mother was sure he was God.

But then there were 3 equally good arguments that Jesus could have been Italian:
1. He talked with his hands.
2. He had wine with every meal.
3. He used olive oil.

But then there were 3 equally good arguments that Jesus could have been a Californian:
1. He never cut his hair.
2. He walked around barefoot all the time.
3. He started a new religion.

But then there were 3 equally good arguments that Jesus could have been Irish:
1. He never got married.
2. He was always telling stories.
3. He loved green pastures.

But the most compelling evidence of all, 3 proofs that Jesus could have been a woman:
1. He fed a crowd at a moment's notice when there was no food.
2. He kept trying to get a message across to a bunch of men who just didn't get it.

3. And even when he was dead, HE HAD TO GET UP BECAUSE THERE WAS MORE WORK TO DO.

Amen

TOP TEN REASONS A
HANDGUN IS BETTER THAN A WOMAN

10. You can trade an old .44 for two new 22's.

9. You can keep one handgun at home and have another for when you're on the road.

8. If you admire a friend's handgun, and tell him, he will probably let you try it out a few times.

7. Your primary handgun doesn't mind if you have a backup.

6. Your handgun will stay with you even if you're out of ammo.

5. A handgun doesn't take up a lot of closet space.

4. Handguns function normally every day of the month.

3. A handgun doesn't ask "do these new grips make me look fat?"

2. A handgun doesn't mind if you go to sleep after you use it.

And the number one way that a handgun is better than a woman:

1. You can buy a silencer for a handgun.

RED SOX – START SPREADING THE NEWS

'Twas a night in October
In the house that Ruth built.
All the New York fans were praying
That their team would not wilt.

They looked at the Red Sox
And it sure gave them fits
Long hair, beards and attitudes
What a bunch of misfits!

George bought the champagne
For the post-game celebration.
'Let's flaunt our success
In front of all Red Sox nation!"

But the Sox had their own plan
And that's never to quit.
Just keep hanging in there
For that game-winning hit.

Now, if you listen to Maisano
.. or Conca … or Phil
You'd think all of the Red Sox
Were over the hill.

Big Papi struck early
With a homer to right.
It looks like the start
Of a historical night.

It was on 'The Mick's birthday
He would have been seventy-three
The Sox paid their respects
With their own hitting spree.

The Disciple named Damon
Like Paul Revere's ride at night
Sent a message through the Bronx
With his grand slam to right.

The Yankees got one back
Thanks to a single by Jeter
But the Disciple crushed another
To make the score sweeter.

While Damon came on as
One of the most unlikely heroes
The Bombers were too stunned
To put up anything by zeroes.

Then Bellhorn joined the fun
When he said 'What the heck'
As he turned on a fastball
That landed in the upper deck.

As I bask in this victory
With a glass of red vino
Could see have finally dispelled
The curse of the Bambino?

Now this comeback by Boston
May have A-Rod and Jeter in tears
But, come on, we deserve it
It's been eighty-six years!

With those fat, heavy wallets
It should really be no mystery
That this Yankee team will be remembered
As the biggest joke in sports history.

Now listen up, Yankee fans
I think you should hear
That the NY on your pinstripes

Only stands for "Next Year"!!

MEDICAL FUNERAL

A cardiologist died and was given an elaborate funeral. A huge heart covered in flowers stood behind the casket during the service. Following the eulogy, the heart opened, and the casket rolled inside. The heart then closed, sealing the doctor in the beautiful heart forever.

At that point one of the mourners burst into laughter. When all eyes stared at him, he said, "I'm sorry, I was just thinking of my own funeral … I'm a gynecologist."

That's when the proctologist fainted.

FBI

The FBI had an opening for an assassin. After all the background checks, interviews, and testing were done there were 3 finalists. Two men and a woman.

For the final test, the FBI agents took one of the men to a large metal door and handed him a gun. "We must know that you will follow your instructions no matter what the circumstances. Inside the room you will find your wife sitting in a chair. Kill her!

The man said, "You can't be serious, I could never shoot my wife." The agent said, "Then you're not the right man for this job. Take your wife and go home."

The second man was given the same instructions. He took the gun and went into the room. All was quiet for about 5 minutes. The man came out with tears in his eyes. "I tried, but I can't kill my wife." The agent said, "You don't have what it takes. Take your wife and go home."

Finally, it was the woman's turn. She was given the same instructions, to kill her husband. She took the gun and went into the room. Shots were heard, one after another. They heard screaming, crashing, banging on the walls. After a few minutes, all was quiet. The door opened slowly and there stood the woman. She wiped the sweat from her brow.

"This gun is loaded with blanks" she said. "I had to beat him to death with the chair."

HURRICANE STRESS

Hurricane stress is real. Let me describe some of the causes. I have been without power since last Saturday the 24th. I have spent a small fortune on a generator, chainsaws, electric cable, gas cans, etc. Here is a chronicle of a now typical day.

Sound of window air conditioner goes off at midnight. Forgot to fill generator up with gas before I went to bed. Get up and flip light switch so I can find flashlight (DUH).

Open door to hallway. Humidity is 111%. Glasses steam up. Trip over black lab sleeping crossways in hall in dark.

Spill gas in shoe while filling generator. Start generator. Door is closed behind me and locked. Find key in secret hiding place. Reset clock on coffee pot. Go back to room, dog gives me a snarling warning growl as I step over him. Wake up wife to reset alarm clock. She also gives me a warning growl. Can't go back to sleep, my feet smell like gasoline.

Alarm goes off at 5:00. Shave with cold water. Go out for paper. It's under middle of car in driveway. Crawl under to retrieve. Check lottery number to see if I've won so I can move to somewhere where there are no hurricanes. Not winner.

Look for something to eat that doesn't have to be heated. Generator doesn't have enough power to run stove or toaster oven. Look in breadbox, mold reigns from humidity. Salt shaker has now become a salt lick. So has Sweet N Low. Scrape hard powder into coffee cup. Will not dissolve. Begin dreading process of taking cold shower. Linger over paper to postpone shower until last minute.

Go out to feed the cat. Trip over cable running from generator which runs down hall to kitchen and into laundry room where it backfeeds into dryer outlet. Black lab blows by trying to get cat.

Go to shower. Turn handle over to hot side hoping for miracle. None available. Heat momentarily stops. Consider hooking up paddles to generator to restart heat. Realize soap does not wash off as easily with cold water as hot. Wonder how Eskimos wash. Maybe that's why they eat fish, blubber, and other smelly stuff to mask smell.

Dry off. Feet still have hint of gasoline smell. Generator kicks off. Flick on light switch so I can find flashlight. Still doesn't come on (DUH). Oil reservoir is low. Refill. Drip oil on foot. Drop flashlight which goes off … Fumble in dark to start generator. Hit hot muffler. Finally restart. Wash oil off foot with cold water.

Finally ready to go to work. Put empty gas cans in car. Now car smells like gasoline. Neighbor (who does not have a generator) gives me an evil look. Don't know if it's because I have left every light on in house and hers is dark or the noise from the generator kept her up.

It's now 6:30 and I'm off. Now I have to find gas station that has gas and the lines don't stretch around the block. If I'm not in the best of moods first thing when I get to the office, please take the above into consideration. By the way, I have attached a map of the crossing points of Charley, Frances and Jeanne.

MAKE SOMEONE HAPPY

Bill, Hillary and Kerry are flying on Kerry's wife's private jet. Bill looks at Hillary, chuckles and says, "You know, I could throw a $100.00 bill out the window right now and make somebody very happy."

Hillary shrugs her shoulders and says, "Well, I could throw ten $10.00 bills out the window and make 10 people very happy."

Kerry says, "Of course then, I could throw on-hundred $1.00 bills out the window and make a hundred people happy."

The pilot rolls her eyes, looks at all of them and says to her co-pilot, "Such Big Shots back there ... Heck, I could throw all of them out the window and make millions happy."

THE YEAR'S BEST HEADLINES OF 2004

- "Crack found on Governor's Daughter." (Imagine that!)

- "Something went wrong in jet crash, expert says." (No, really?)

- "Police begins campaign to run down jaywalkers." (Now that's taking things a bit far!)

- "Is there a ring of debris around Uranus?" (Not if you wipe thoroughly!)

- "Panda mating fails; veterinarian takes over." (What a guy!)

- "Miners refuse to work after death." (No-good-for-nothin' lazy so-and-so's!)

- "Juvenile court to try shooting defendant." (See if that works any better than a fair trial!)

- "War dims hope for peace." (I can see where it might have that effect!)

- "If strike isn't settled quickly, it may last awhile." (You think?)

- "Cold wave linked to temperatures." (Who would have thought?)

- "Enfield (London) couple slain; police suspect homicide." (They may be on to something!)

- "Red tape holds up new bridges." (You mean there's something stronger than duct tape?)

- "Man struck by lightning faces battery charge." (He probably is the battery charge!)

- "New study of obesity looks for larger test group." (Weren't they fat enough?)

- "Astronaut takes blame for gas in spacecraft." (Now that's a stand-up kinda guy!)

- "Kids make nutritious snacks." (Taste like chicken?)

- "Local high school dropouts cut in half." (Chainsaw Massacre all over again!)

- And the winner is … "Typhoon rips through cemetery; hundreds dead."

THE PRIEST, THE PREACHER AND THE RABBI

A priest, a Pentecostal preacher and a Rabbi all served as chaplains to the students of Northern Michigan University in Marquette. They would get together two or three times a week for coffee and to talk shop.

One day, someone made the comment that preaching to people isn't really all that hard. A real challenge would be to preach to a bear. One thing led to another and they decided to do an experiment. They would all go out into the woods, find a bear, preach to it, and attempt to convert it.

Father Flannery, who has his arm in a sling, is on crutches, and has various bandages, goes first. "Well," he says, "I went into the woods to find me a bear. And when I found him I began to read to him from the Catechism. Well, that bear wanted nothing to do with me and began to slap me around. So I quickly grabbed my holy water, sprinkle him and, Holy Mary Mother of God, he became as gentle as a lamb. The bishop is coming out next week to give him first communion and confirmation."

Reverend Billy Bob spoke next. He was in a wheelchair, with an arm and both legs in casts, and an IV drip. In his best fire and brimstone oratory he claimed, "Well brothers, you know that we don't sprinkle! I went out and found me a bear. And then I began to read to my bear from God's HOLY WORD! But that bear wanted nothing to do with me. So I took hold of him and we began to wrestle. We wrestled down one hill, up another and down another until we came to a creek. So I quick dunked him and baptized his hairy soul. And just like you said, he became as gentle as a lamb. We spent the rest of the day praising Jesus."

They both looked down at the rabbi, who was lying in a hospital bed. He was in a body cast and traction with IV's and monitors running in and out of him. He was in bad shape. The rabbi looks up and says,

"Looking back on it, circumcision may not have been the best way to start."

MEN VS. WOMEN

A man will pay $2 for an item that costs $1 if he wants it. A woman will pay $1 for a $2 item that she doesn't want because it's on sale.

A woman worries about the future until she gets a husband. A man never worries about the future until he gets a wife.

A successful man is one who makes more money than his wife can spend. A successful woman is one who can find that man.

To be happy with a man, you must understand him a lot and love him a little. To be happy with a woman, you must love her a lot and don't expect to understand her at all.

Married men live longer than single men, but married men are a lot more willing to die.

Any married man can forget his past mistakes: there's no reason for two people to keep track of the same things.

A woman marries a man expecting him to change, and he doesn't. A man marries a woman expecting her not to change, and she does.

A woman has the last word in any argument. Anything a man says after that is the beginning of a new argument.

PUNDAMENTAL

It seems that Leonard Bernstein was conducting a new recording of Beethoven's 9th Symphony when the sound recording equipment broke.

The musicians were given a 2 hour break during which the entire bass section and two French horn players went to a local bar and became intoxicated.

When the recording resumed, Bernstein dropped the music score book and loose pages scattered everywhere.

An assistant took string and bound the score back together again. At that moment, the two French horn players passed out and as Bernstein lifted his baton. If you were Leonard what would you do in this situation?

IT WAS THE BOTTOM OF THE NINTH, THE SCORE WAS TIED, THERE WERE TWO OUT, AND THE BASSES WERE LOADED.

IF MEN TRULY RULED THE WORLD

Breaking up would be a lot easier. A smack on the behind and a "Nice hustle, you'll get 'em next time" would pretty much do it.

Valentine's Day would be moved to February 29th so it would only occur in leap years.

On Groundhog Day, if you saw your shadow, you'd get the day off to go drinking. Anniversaries too.

St. Patrick's Day, however, would remain exactly the same. But it would be celebrated every month on the 17th.

The only show opposite "Monday Night Football" would be "Monday Night Football" from a different camera angle.

Instead of 'beer-belly', you'd get "beer-biceps".

Tanks would be far easier to rent.

Birth control would come in ale or lager.

Garbage would take itself out.

The funniest guy in the office would get to be CEO.

People would never talk about how fresh they felt.

Daisy Duke shorts would never go out of style again.

Every man would get four, real Get Out of Jail Free cards.

Telephones would cut off after 30 seconds of conversation.

Instead of a fancy, expensive engagement ring, you could present your wife-to-be with a giant foam hand that said "You're #1!"

When your wife/girlfriend really needed to talk to you during the game, she'd appear in a little box in the corner of the screen during a time-out.

Nodding and looking at your watch would be deemed as an acceptable response to "I Love You".

"Sorry I'm late, but I lost all track of time playing poker last night," would be an acceptable excuse for tardiness.

At the end of the workday, a whistle would blow and you would jump out of your window and slide down the tail of a brontosaurus and right into your car like Fred Flintstone.

Lifeguards could remove citizens from beaches for violating the 'public ugliness" ordinance.

Hallmark would make "Sorry, what was your name again?" cards.

2005

NEW YORK CITY BOARD OF EDUCATION

Revised High School Math Proficiency Exam
Name_____ Date _____
Gang Name _____

1. Jose has 2 ounces of cocaine. If he sells an 8 ball to Antonio for $320 and 2 grams to Juan for $85 per gram, what is the street value of the rest of his hold?

2. Rufus pimps 3 hoes. If the price is $85 per trick, how many tricks per day must each ho turn to support Rufus' $800 per day crack habit?

3. Jerome wants to cut the pound of cocaine he bought for $40,000 to make 20% profit. How many ounces will he need?

4. Willie gets $200 for a stolen BMW, $150 for stealing a Corvette, and $100 for a 4x4. If he steals 1 BMW, 2 Corvettes, and 3 4x4's, how many more Corvettes must he steal to have $900?

5. Raoul got 6 yeas for murder. He also got $10,000 for the hit. If his common-law wife spends $100 per month, how much money will be left when he gets out?

6. ** Extra credit question: How much more time will be get for killing the ho that spent his money??

7. If an average can of spray paint covers 22 square feet and the average letter is 3 square feet, how many letters can be sprayed with 3 eight ounce cans of spray paint?

8. Hector knocked up 3 girls in the gang. There are 27 girls in his gang. What is the exact percentage of girls Hector knocked up?

9. Bernie is a lookout for the gang. Bernie has a boa constrictor that eats 3 small rats per week at a cost of $5 per rat. If Bernie

makes $700 a weed as a lookout, how many weeks can he feed the boa with one weeks salary?

10. Billy steals Joe's skateboard. As Billy skates away at 35 mph, Joe loads his 357 Magnum. It is takes Joe 20 seconds to load his Magnum, how far away will Billy be when he gets whacked?

GIRLS' NIGHT OUT

Two women who had been friends for years, decided to go for a Girls' Night Out, and were decidedly over-enthusiastic on the martinis. Incredibly drunk and walking home, they needed to use the bathroom.

They were very near a cemetery and one of them suggested they wiz behind a headstone. The first woman had nothing to dry herself with so she decided she'd take off her panties, use them, and then throw them away.

The second woman, however, was wearing rather expensive underwear and didn't want to ruin hers, but was lucky to salvage a large ribbon from a wreath that was on one of the graves. She dried herself with the ribbon.

After finishing, they then made off for home. The next day, the first woman's husband phoned the other husband and said, "This girls' night out thing has got to stop right now. My wife came home last night without her panties."

"That's nothing," said the other husband. "Mine came home with a card stuck to her ass that said, 'From all of us at the fire station. We'll never forget you.'"

TRUE LESSONS

Bill Gates gave a speech at a High School about 11 things they did not and will not learn in school. He talks about how feel-good, politically-correct teaching created a generation of kids with no concept of reality and how this concept set them up for failure in the real world. For any of us who work with kids or come across kids during our day, the following is so true.

1. Life is not fair, get use to it.

2. The world won't care about your self-esteem. The world will expect you to accomplish something before you feel good about yourself.

3. You will not make $60,000 a year right out of high school. You won't be a vice-president with a car phone until you earn both.

4. If you think your teacher is tough, wait till you get a boss.

5. If you mess up, it's not your parents' fault, so don't whine about your mistakes, learn from them.

6. Before you were born, your parents weren't as boring as they now are. They got that way paying your bills, cleaning your clothes and listening to you talk about how cool you thought you were. So before you save the rain forest from the parasites of your parent's generation, try delousing the closet in your own room.

7. Flipping burgers is not beneath your dignity. Your grandparents had a different word for flipping burgers – they called it Opportunity.

8. Your school may have done away with winners and losers, but life has not! In some schools they have abolished failing grades and they'll give you as many times as you want to get the right answer. This doesn't bear the slightest resemblance to anything is real life.

9. Life is not divided into semesters. You don't get summers off and very few employers are interested in helping you "find yourself." Do that on your own time.

10. Television is not real life. In real life, people actually have to leave the coffee shop and go to jobs.

11. Be nice to nerds! Chances are you'll end up working for one.

PIG

Man driving down the road. Woman driving up same road.
They pass each other.
Woman yells out window, "PIG!"
Man yells out the window, "BITCH!"
Man rounds next curve, crashes into a huge pig in the middle of the road.
Thought for the Day: If only men would listen.

SLAP YOUR CO-WORKER DAY IS COMING

Tomorrow is the official Slap your Irritating Co-Worker Holiday. Do you have a co-worker who talks nonstop about nothing, working your last nerve with tedious and boring details that you don't give a damn about? Do you have a co-worker who always screws up stuff creating more work for you? Do you have a co-worker who kisses so much booty, you can look in their mouth and see what your boss had for lunch? Do you have a co-worker who is sooo obnoxious, when he/she enters a room, everyone else clears it? Well, on behalf of Ike Turner, I am so very very glad to officially announce tomorrow as SLAP YOUR IRRITATING CO-WORKER DAY! There are rules you must follow though:

- You can only slap one person per hour – no more.

- You can slap the same person again if they irritate you again in the same day.

- You are allowed to hold someone down as other co-workers take their turns slapping the irritant.

- No weapons are allowed ... other than going upside somebody's head with a stapler or a hole-puncher.

- CURSING IS MANDATORY! After you have slapped the recipient, your "assault" must be followed with something like, "cause I'm sick of your stupid-a$$ always messing up stuff!"

- If questioning by a supervisor (or police, if the supervisor is the irritant), you are allowed to LIE, LIE, LIE! Now, study the rules, break out your list of folks that you want to slap the living day lights out of and get to slapping ... and have a great day.

(NO TITLE)

A 3-year old boy examined his testicles while taking a bath. "Mom," he asked, "are these my brains?"
"Not yet," she replied.

YOU MIGHT BE A REDNECK IF:
Y'ALL KNOW WHO YA' ARE....

We have enjoyed the redneck jokes for years. It's time to take a reflective look at the core beliefs of a culture that values home, family, country and God. If I had to stand before a dozen terrorists who threaten my life, I'd choose a half dozen or so rednecks to back me up. Tire irons, squirrel guns and grit – that's what rednecks are made of. I hope you feel the same.

You might be a Redneck if:

1. It never occurred to you to be offended by the phrase, "One nation, under God."
2. You've never protested about seeing the 10 Commandments posted in public places.
3. You still say "Christmas" instead of "Winter Festival."
4. You remove your hat and bow your head when anyone prays.
5. You stand and place your hand over your heart when they play the National Anthem.
6. You treat Viet Nam vets with great respect, and always have.
7. You've never burned an American flag, but would kick someone's tail that did.
8. You know what you believe and you aren't afraid to say so, no matter who is listening.
9. You respect your elders and expect your kids to do the same.
10. You'd give your last dollar to a friend.

WHAT MY MOTHER TAUGHT ME

1. My mother taught me "TO APPRECIATE A JOB WELL DONE." "If you're going to kill each other, do it outside. I just finished cleaning."

2. My mother taught me RELIGION. "You better pray that will come out of the carpet."

3. My mother taught me about TIME TRAVEL. "If you don't straighten up, I'm going to knock you into the middle of next week."

4. My mother taught me LOGIC. "Because I said so, that's why."

5. My mother taught me MORE LOGIC. "If you fall out of that swing and break your neck, you're not going to the store with me."

6. My mother taught me FORESIGHT. "Make sure you wear clean underwear, in case you're in an accident."

7. My mother taught me IRONY. "Keep crying, and I'll give you something to cry about."

8. My mother taught me about science of OSMOSIS. "Shut your mouth and eat your supper."

9. My mother taught me about CONTORTIONISM." "Will you look at that dirt on the back of your neck!"

10. My mother taught me about STAMINA. "You'll sit there until all that spinach is gone."

11. My mother taught me about WEATHER. "This room of yours looks as if a tornado went through it."

12. My mother taught me about HYPOCRICY. "If I told you once, I've told you a million times, don't exaggerate!"

13. My mother taught me the CIRCLE OF LIFE. "I brought you into this world, and I can take you out."

14. My mother taught me about BEHAVIOR MODIFICATIONS. "Stop acting like your father."

15. My mother taught me about ENVY. "There are millions of less fortunate children in this world who don't have wonderful parents like you do."

16. My mother taught me about ANTICIPATION. "Just wait until we get home."

17. My mother taught me about RECEIVING. "You are going to get it when you get home."

18. My mother taught me MEDICAL SCIENCE. "If you don't stop crossing your eyes, they are going to freeze that way."

19. My mother taught me EPS. "Put your sweater on; don't you think I know when you are cold."

20. My mother taught me HUMOR. "When that lawn mower cuts off your toes, don't come running to me."

21. My mother taught me HOW TO BECOME AN ADULT. "If you don't eat your vegetables, you'll never grow up."

22. My mother taught me GENETICS. "You're just like your father."

23. My mother taught me about my ROOTS. "Shut that door behind you. Do you think you were born in a barn?"

24. My mother taught me WISDOM. "When you get to be my age, you'll understand."

25. And my favorite: my mother taught me about JUSTICE. "One day you'll have kids, and I hope they turn out just like you."

ONLY IN AMERICA

Only in America … do drugstores make the sick walk all the way to the back of the store to get their prescriptions while healthy people can buy cigarettes at the front.

Only in America … do people order double cheeseburgers, large fries, and a diet coke.

Only in America … do we leave cars worth thousands of dollars in the driveway and put the useless junk in the garage.

Only in America … do banks leave both doors open and then chain the pens to the counters.

Only in America … do we buy hot dogs in packages of ten and buns in packages of eight.

Only in America … do we use the word 'politics' to describe the process so well: "Poli" in Latin meaning "many" and "tics" meaning "bloodsucking creatures."

Only in America … do they have drive-up ATM machines with Braille lettering.

EVER WONDER ...

Why the sun lightens our hair, but darkens our skin?

Why women can't put on mascara with their mouth closed?

Why don't you ever see the headline "Psychic Wins Lottery"?

Why is "abbreviated" such a long word?

Why is it that doctors call what they do "practice"?

Why is lemon juice made with artificial flavor, and dishwashing liquid made with real lemons?

Why is the man who invests all your money called a broker?

Why is the time of day with the slowest traffic called rush hour?

Why isn't there mouse-flavored cat food?

Why didn't Noah swat those two mosquitoes?

Why do they sterilize the needle for lethal injections?

You know that indestructible black box that is used on airplanes? Why don't they make the whole plane out of that stuff?!

Why don't sheep shrink when it rains?

Why are they called apartments when they are all stuck together?

If con is the opposite of pro, is Congress the opposite of progress?

If flying is so safe, why do they call the airport the terminal?

CYANIDE

A lady walks into a drug store and tells the pharmacist she needs some cyanide.

The pharmacist asked, "Why in the world do you need cyanide?" The lady then explained she needed it to poison her husband.

The pharmacist's eyes got big and he said, "Lord, have mercy! I can't give you cyanide to kill your husband! That's against the law. I'll lose my license; they'll throw both of us in jail and all kinds of bad things will happen! Absolutely not – you can NOT have any cyanide!"

The lady reached into her purse and pulled out a picture of her husband in bed with the pharmacist's wife. The pharmacist looked at the picture and replied, "Well, now. You didn't tell me you had a prescription."

(NO TITLE)

Mujibar was trying to get into the USA legally through immigration.

The officer said, "Mujibar, you have passed most of the required tests, but there is one more compulsory language test. Unless you pass it you cannot enter the States."

Mujibar said, "I am ready."

The officer said, "Make a sentence using the words yellow, pink and green.

Mujibar thought for a few minutes and said, "Mister officer, I am ready."

The officer said, "Go ahead."

Mujibar said, "The telephone goes green, green, green, and I pink it up, and say, 'Yellow, this is Mujibar."

Mujibar now lives in a neighborhood near you, and works at a Verizon Help Desk.

THE CAT IN THE HAT ON AGING

I cannot see
I cannot pee
I cannot chew
I cannot screw
Oh my God, what can I do?
My memory shrinks
My hearing stinks
No sense of smell
I look like hell
My mood is bad - can you tell?
My body's drooping
Have trouble pooping
The golden years
Have come at last
The Golden Years
Can kiss my ass.

(NO TITLE)

Babs Miller was bagging some early potatoes for me. I noticed a small boy, delicate of bone and feature, ragged but clean, hungrily apprising a basket of freshly picked green peas.

I paid for my potatoes but was also drawn to the display of fresh green peas. I am a pushover for creamed peas and new potatoes. Pondering the peas, I couldn't help overhearing the conversation between Mr. Miller and the ragged boy next to me.

"Hello Barry, how are you today?"

"H'lo, Mr. Miller. Fine, thank ya, Jus' admirin' them peas. Sure look good."

They are good, Barry, How's you Ma?"

"Fine. Gittin' stronger alla' time."

"Good. Anything I can help you with?"

"No, sir. Jus' admirin' them peas."

"Would you like to take some home?"

"No, sir. Got nuthin' to pay for 'em with."

"Well, what have you to trade me for some of those peas?"

All I got's my prize marble here."

"Is that right? Let me see it."

"Here 'tis. She's a dandy."

"I can see that. Hmmmmm, only thing is this one is blue and I sort of go for red. Do you have a red one like this at home?"

"Not zackley, but almost."

"Tell you what. Take this sack of peas home with you and next trip this way let me look at that red marble."

"Sure will, Thanks Mr. Miller."

Mrs. Miller, who had been standing nearby, came over to help me. With a smile she said, "There are two other boys like him in our community, all three are in very poor circumstances. Jim just loves to bargain with them for peas, apples, tomatoes, or whatever. When they come back with their red marbles, and they always do, he decides he doesn't like red after all and he sends them home with a bag of produce for a green marble or an orange one, perhaps."

I left the stand smiling to myself, impressed with this man. A short time later I moved to Colorado, but I never forgot the story of this man, the boys, and their bartering.

Several years went by, each more rapid than the previous one. Just recently, I had occasion to visit some old friends in that Idaho community and while I was there I learned that Mr. Miller had died. They were having his viewing that evening and knowing my friends wanted to go, I agreed to accompany them. Upon arrival at the mortuary, we fell into line to meet the relatives of the deceased and to offer whatever words of comfort we could.

Ahead of us in line were three young men. One was in an army uniform and the other two wore nice haircuts, dark suits and white shirts … all very professional looking.

They approached Mrs. Miller, standing composed and smiling by her husband's casket. Each of the young men hugged her, kissed her on the cheek, spoke briefly with her and moved on to the casket.

Her misty light blue eyes followed them as, one-by-one, each young man stopped briefly and placed his own warm hand over the cold pale hand in the casket. Each left the mortuary awkwardly, wiping his eyes.

Our turn came to meet Mrs. Miller. I told her who I was and mentioned the story she had told me about the marbles. With her eyes glistening, she took my hand and led me to the casket.

"Those three young men who just left were the boys I told you about. They just told me how they appreciated the things Jim "traded" them. Now, at last, when Jim could not change his mind about color or size … they came to pay their debt."

"We've never had a great deal of the wealth of this world," she confided, "but right now, Jim would consider himself the richest man in Idaho."

With loving gentleness she lifted the lifeless fingers of her deceased husband. Resting underneath were three exquisitely shined red marbles.

Moral: We will not be remembered by our words, but by our kind deeds. Life is not measured by the breaths we take, but by the moments that take our breath.

Today, I wish you a day of ordinary miracles … A fresh pot of coffee you didn't make yourself …An unexpected phone call from an old friend … Green stoplights on your way to work … The fastest line at the grocery store … A good sing-along on the radio … Your keys right where you left them.

UP YER DOSAGE!

By following the simple advice I heard on a Dr. Phil Show, I have finally found inner peace. Dr. Phil proclaimed the way to achieve inner peace is to finish all the things you have started.

So I looked around my house to see things I started and hadn't finished; and, before leaving the house this morning I finished off a bottle of Merlot, a bottle of Chardonnay, a bottle of Baileys, a bottle of Kahlua, a package of Oreo's, a pot of coffee, the rest of the Cheesecake, some Saltines and a box of Godiva Chocolates.

You have no idea how freaking good I feel.

A bus stops and 2 men get on, one is Italian. They sit down and engage in an animated conversation

The lady sitting next to them ignores them at first, but her attention is galvanized when she hears one of them say the following:

"Emma come first. Den I come. Den two asses come together. I come once-a-more. Two asses, they come together again. I come again and pee twice. Then I come one lasta time."

"You foul-mouthed sex obsessed swine," retorted the lady indignantly. In this country…we don't speak aloud in public places about our sex lives."
"Hey, coola down lady," said the man. "Who talkin' about a sex? I'm a justa tellin' my frienda how to spell 'Mississippi'."

I've got $5.00 that says you're gonna read this again!

JESUS AND FINKELSTEIN

Jesus was wandering around Jerusalem when He decided that He really needed a new robe. After looking around for a while, He saw a sign for Finkelstein, the Tailor. So, He went in and made the necessary arrangements to have Finkelstein prepare a new robe for Him.

A few days later, when the robe was finished, Jesus tried it on and it was a perfect fit! He asked how much He owed. Finkelstein brushed him off: "No, no, no, for the Son of God? There's so charge! However, may I ask for a small favor? Whenever you give a sermon, perhaps you could just mention that your nice new robe was made by Finkelstein, the Tailor?"

Jesus readily agreed and as promised, extolled the virtues of His Finkelstein robe whenever He spoke to the masses. A few months later, while Jesus was again walking through Jerusalem, He happened to walk past Finkelstein's hoop and noted a huge line of people waiting for Finkelstein's robes.

He pushed his way through the crowd to speak to him and as soon as Finkelstein spotted Him he said: "Jesus, Jesus, look what you've done for my business! Would you consider a partnership?"

"Certainly," replied Jesus. "Jesus and Finkelstein it is."

"Oh, no, no," said Finkelstein. "Finkelstein & Jesus. After all, I am the craftsman."

The two of them debated this for some time. Their discussion was long and spirited, but ultimately fruitful and they finally came up with a mutually acceptable compromise.

A few days later, the new sign went up over Finkelstein's shop ... Lord and Taylor.

THE ITALIAN TOMATO GARDEN

The old Italian man lived alone in the country. He wanted to dig his tomato garden, but it was very hard work as the ground was hard. His only son, Vincent, who used to help him, was in prison. The old man wrote a letter to his son and described his predicament.

Dear Vincent:
I am feeling pretty bad because it looks like I won't be able to plant my tomato garden this year. I'm just getting too old to be digging up a garden plot. If you were here, my troubles would be over. I know you would dig the plot for me. Love Dad.

A few days later he received a letter from his son.

Dear Dad:
Not for nothing, but don't dig up that garden. That's where I buried the BODIES. Love Vinnie.

At 4 a.m. the next morning, FBI agents and local police arrived and dug up the entire area without finding any bodies. They apologized to the old man and left. That same day the old man received another letter from his son.

Dear Dad:
Go ahead and plant the tomatoes now. That's the best I could do under the circumstances. Love Vinnie.

NO NURSING HOME FOR ME

About two years ago my wife and I were on a cruise through the western Mediterranean aboard a Princess liner. At dinner we noticed an elderly lady sitting alone along the rail of the grand stairway in the main dining room. I noticed that all the staff, ship officers, waiters, busboys, etc. all seemed very familiar with this lady. I asked our waiter who the lady was, expecting to be told she owned the line, but said he only knew that she had been on board for the last four cruises back to back.

As we left the dining room one evening, I caught her eye and stopped to say hello. We chatted and I said, "I understand you've been on this ship for the last four cruises."

She replied, "Yes, that's true."

I stated, "I don't understand," and she replied without a pause, "It's cheaper than a nursing home."

So, there will be no nursing home in my future. When I get old and feeble, I am going to get on a Princess cruise ship. The average cost for a nursing home is $200 a day. I have checked on reservations at princess and I can get a long term discount and senior discount price of $135 per day.

That leaves $65 a day for:

1. Gratuities which will only be $10 per day.
2. I will have as many as 110 meals a day if I can waddle to the restaurant or I can have room service (which means I can have breakfast in bed every day of the week.)
3. Princess has as many as three swimming pools, a workout room, free washers and dryers and shows every night.
4. They have free toothpaste, razors, soap and shampoo.

5. They will even treat you like a customer, not a patient. An extra $5 worth of tips will have the entire staff scrambling to help you.

6. I will get to meet new people every 7 to 14 days.

7. TV broken? Light bulb needs changing? Need to have the mattress replaced? No problem! They will fix everything and apologize for your inconvenience.

8. Clean sheets and towels every day and you don't even have to ask for them.

9. If you fall in the nursing home and break a hip, you are on Medicare. If you fall and break a hip on the Princess ship, they will upgrade you to a suite for the rest of your life.

Now hold on for the best! Do you want to see South America, the Panama Canal, Tahiti, Australia, New Zealand, Asia or name where you want to go … Princess will have a ship ready to go. So don't look for me in a nursing home.

P.S. And don't forget, when you die, they just dump you over the side at no charge.

THE GOOD PRIEST'S ADVICE.
THOSE CATHOLICS KNOW THEIR BUSINESS

A businessman was in a great deal of trouble. His business was failing, he had put everything he had into the business, he owed everybody – it was so bad he was even contemplating suicide. As a last resort he went to a priest and poured out his story of tears and woe. When he had finished, the priest said. "Here's what I want you to do: Put a beach chair and your Bible in your car and drive down to the beach. Take the beach chair and the Bible to the water's edge, sit down in the beach chair, and put the Bible in your lap. Open the Bible; the wind will rifle the pages, but finally the open Bible will come to rest on a page. Look down at the page and read the first thing you see. That will be your answer that will tell you what to do."

A year later the businessman went back to the priest and brought his wife and children with him. The man was in a new custom-tailored suit, his wife in a mink coat, the children shining. The businessman pulled an envelope stuffed with money out of his pocket, gave it to the priest as a donation in thanks for his advice.

The priest recognized the benefactor, and was curious. "You did as I suggested?" he asked.

"Absolutely," replied the businessman.

"You went to the beach?"

"Absolutely."

"You sat in a beach chair with the Bible in your lap?"

"Absolutely."

"You let the pages rifle until they stopped?"

"Absolutely."

"And what were the first words you saw?"

"Chapter 11."

CHAIN LETTERS

I want to thank all of you who have taken the time and trouble to send me your damn chain letters over the past few years. Yes, thank you, thank you, thank you from the bottom of what's left of my heart for making me feel safe, secure, blessed and wealthy.

Because of your concern … I no longer can drink Coca Cola because it can remove toilet stains.

I no longer drink Pepsi or Dr. Pepper since the people who make these products are atheists who refuse to put "Under God" on their cans.

I no longer use Saran wrap in the microwave because it causes cancer.

I no longer check the coin return on pay phones because I could be pricked with a needle infected with AIDS.

I no longer use cancer-causing deodorants even though I smell like a water buffalo on a hot day.

I no longer use margarine because it's one molecule away from being plastic.

I no longer go to shopping malls because someone will drug me with a perfume sample and rob me.

I no longer receive packages from UPS or FedEx since they are actually Al Qaeda in disguise.

I no longer answer the phone because someone will ask me to dial a stupid number for which I will get a phone bill from hell with calls to Jamaica, Uganda, Singapore, and Uzbekistan.

I no longer eat KFC because their chickens are actually horrible mutant freaks with no eyes or feathers.

I no longer date the opposite sex because they will take my kidneys and leave me taking a nap in a bathtub full of ice.

I no longer buy expensive cookies from Neiman Marcus since I now have their recipe.

I no longer worry about my soul because I have 363,214 angels looking out for me and St. Theresa's novena has granted my every wish.

Thanks to you, I have learned that God only answers my prayers if I forward and email to seven of my friends and make a wish within five minutes. (Geez, the Bible did not mention it works that way!)

I no longer have any savings because I gave it to a sick girl who is about to die in the hospital (for the 1,378,258th time.)

I no longer have any money at all, but that will change once I receive the $15,000 that Microsoft and AOL are sending me for participating in their special e-mail program.

Yes, I want to thank all of you sooooooooo much for looking out for me!

I will now return the favor.

If you don't send this e-mail to at least 1200 people in the next 60 seconds, a large bird with diarrhea will crap on your head at 5:00 PM this afternoon and the fleas of a thousand camels will infest your armpits.

I know this will occur because it actually happened to a friend of a friend of a friend of a friend of a friend of my next door neighbor's ex-mother-in-law's 8th husband's 2nd cousin's 3rd husband's ex-wife's mother's beautician!

Have a great day!

BAD DAY AT THE OFFICE?

When you have a "I hate my job" day, try this:

1. On your way home from work, stop at your pharmacy and go to the thermometer section.

2. You will need to purchase a rectal thermometer made by "Johnson and Johnson." Be very sure you get this brand.

3. When you get home, lock your doors, draw the drapes, and disconnect the phone, so you will not be disturbed during your therapy.

4. Change to very comfortable clothing, such as a tracksuit and lie down on your bed.

5. Open the package and remove the thermometer. Carefully place it on the bedside table so that it will not become chipped or broken.

6. Take out the material that comes with the thermometer and read it. You will notice that in small print there is a statement: "Every rectal thermometer made by Johnson and Johnson is personally tested."

7. Now close your eyes and repeat out loud five times: "I am so glad I do not work for quality control at the Johnson and Johnson Company."

WHO MAKES BEST PATIENTS?

Five surgeons are discussing who are the best patients to operate on: The first surgeon says, "I like to see accountants on my operating table because when you open them up, everything inside is numbered."

The second responds, "Yeah, but you should try electricians! Everything inside them is color coded."

The third surgeon chimes in: "No, I rally think librarians are the best; everything inside them is in alphabetical order."

The fourth surgeon chimes in: "You know, I like construction workers. Those guys always understand when you have a few parts left over at the end, and when the job takes longer than you said it would."

But the fifth surgeon shut them all up when he observed: "You're all wrong. Politicians are the easiest to operate on. There's no guts, no heart, no balls, no brains and no spine, and the head and the ass are interchangeable."

GEORGE CARLIN'S VIEWS ON AGING

Do you realize that the only time in our lives when we like to get old is when we're kids? If you're less than 10 years old, you're so excited about aging that you think in fractions.

"How old are you?" "I'm four and a half!" You're never thirty-six and a half. You're four and a half, going on five!

THAT'S THE KEY.

You get into your teens, now they can't hold you back. You jump to the next number ... or even a few ahead. How old are you?" "I'm gonna be 16! You could be 13, but hey, you're gonna be 16!

And then the greatest day of your life you become 21. **Even the words sound like a ceremony .. YOU become 21.**

Yesssss! But then you turn 30. Oooohhh what happened there? Makes you sound like bad milk. He TURNED; we had to throw him out.

There's no fun now. You're just a sour-dumpling. What's wrong? What's changed? You **become** 21, you **turned** 30, then you're **PUSHING** 40.

Whoa! Put on the brakes ... it's all slipping away. Before you know it, you **REACHED 50** and your dreams are gone

But wait !! You make it to 60. You didn't think you would. So you **become** 21, **turn** 30, **push** 40, **reach** 50 and **make it to 60.**

You've built up so much speed that you **HIT 70!** After that's it's a day-by-day thing; you hit Wednesday!

You get into your 80's and every day is a complete cycle; you **hit** lunch, **turn** 4:30; you **reach** bedtime.

And it doesn't end there. Into the 90's, you start going backwards ... **"I was just 92."**

Then a strange thing happens. IF you make it over 100, you become a little kid again. **"I'm 100 and a half!"**

May you all make it to a healthy 100 and a half!!

COULD NOT HELP MYSELF

Two things Navy SEALS are always taught:
1. Keep your priorities in order.
2. Know when to act without hesitation.

A College professor, an avowed atheist and active in the ACLU, was teaching his class. He shocked several of his students when he flatly stated that for once and for all he was going to prove there was no God. Addressing the ceiling he shouted:

"God, if you are real, then I want you to knock me off this platform. I'll give you exactly 15 minutes!!!" The lecture room fell silent. You could hear a pin drop. Ten minutes went by. "I'm waiting God, if you're real, knock me off this platform!!"

Again after about 5 minutes, the professor taunted God saying, "Here I am, God!!! I'm still waiting!!!"

His count down got down to the last couple of seconds when a SEAL, just released from the Navy after serving in Afghanistan and Iraq, and newly registered in the class, walked up to the Professor. The SEAL hit him full force in the face, and sent the Professor tumbling from his lofty platform.

The Professor was out cold!! The students were stunned and shocked. They began to babble in confusion. The SEAL nonchalantly took his seat in the front row and sat down. The class looked at him and fell silent.... Waiting. Eventually, the professor came to and was noticeably shaken. He looked at the SEAL in the front row. When the professor regained his senses and could speak he asked: "What is the matter with you?! Why did you do that!?"

"God was really busy, protecting America's soldiers, who are protecting your right to say stupid things and act like an @#%*!!! So he sent me!!!"

ITALIAN BREAD

Two old guys, one 80 and one 87, were sitting on their usual park bench one morning. The 87-year old had just finished his morning jog and wasn't even short of breath.

The 80-year old was amazed at his friend's stamina and asked him what he did to have so much energy. The 87-year old said; "Well, I eat Italian bread every day. It keeps your energy level high and you'll have great stamina with the ladies."

So, on the way home, the 80-year old stops at the bakery. As he was looking around, the lady asked if he needed any help.

He said, "Do you have any Italian bread?"

She said, "Yes, there's a whole shelf of it. Would you like some?"

He said, "I want 5 loaves."

She said, "My goodness, 5 loaves...don't you think by the time you get to the 5th loaf, it'll be hard?"

He replied, "Holy crap...! Everybody in the world knows about this Italian bread thing but me...?!"

USE IT OR LOSE IT

Wife comes home early from work one day only to find her husband in bed with a strange woman.

She says, "That's it, I'm leaving and never coming back."

He says, "Don't you at least want to hear my explanation?"

She shrugs and says, "Fine, let's hear your story. And this had better be good!"

He says, "Well, I'm driving along the street, when I see this young lady in torn clothes, no shoes, all muddy and crying. I took pity on her and asked if she would like to get cleaned up in my house. She climbed into my truck and I brought her home. She took a shower, I gave her the underwear that doesn't fit you anymore, the silk blouse and slacks that I bought you two years ago that you wore once, the $150 Nike running shoes you bought and wore only twice. I even gave her some of the roast beef you had in the fridge that you never served me. I showed her to the door.

"She was so grateful, for all these things, and she thanked me profusely. But then, as she was about to leave she turned around and asked me … 'Is there anything else your wife doesn't use anymore?'"

THINGS YOU MAY NOT KNOW

1. Money isn't made out of paper; it's made out of cotton.

2. The 57 on Heinz ketchup bottle represents the varieties of pickle the company once made.

3. Your stomach produces a new layer of mucus every two weeks – otherwise it will digest itself.

4. The Declaration of Independence was written on hemp paper.

5. The dot over the letter 'I' is called a "tittle".

6. A raisin dropped in a glass of fresh champagne will bounce up and down continuously from the bottom of the glass to the top.

7. Susan Lucci is the daughter of Phyllis Diller.

8. A duck's quack doesn't echo … no one knows why.

9. 40% of McDonald's profits come from the sales of Happy Meals.

10. Every person has a unique tongue print.

11. 315 entries in Webster's 1996 Dictionary were misspelled.

12. The 'spot' on 7UP comes from its inventor who had red eyes. He was albino.

13. On average, 12 newborns will be given to the wrong parents daily.

14. During the chariot scene in 'Ben Hur' a small red car can be seen in the distance.

15. Warren Beatty and Shirley McLain are brother and sister.

16. Chocolate affects a dog's heart and nervous system; a few ounces will kill a small size dog.

17. Orcas (killer whales) kill sharks by torpedoing up into the shark's stomach from underneath, causing the shark to explode.

18. Most lipstick contains fish scales.

19. Donald Duck comics were banned from Finland because he doesn't wear pants.

20. Ketchup was sold in the 1830's as medicine.

21. Upper and lower case letters are named 'upper' and 'lower' because in the time when all original print had to be set in individual letters, and 'upper case' letters were stored in the case on top of the case that stored the smaller, 'lower case' letters.

22. Leonardo da Vinci could write with one hand and draw with the other at the same time.

23. Because metals were scarce, the Oscars given out during Would War II were made of wood.

24. There are no clocks in Las Vegas gambling casinos.

25. The name Wendy was made up for the book Peter Pan, there was never a recorded Wendy before!

26. There are no words in the dictionary that rhyme with: orange, purple, and silver!

27. Leonardo da Vinci invented scissors. Also, it took him 10 years to paint Mona Lisa's lips.

28. A tiny amount of liquor on a scorpion will make it instantly go mad and sting itself to death.

29. The mask used by Michael Myers in the original "Halloween" was a Captain Kirk mask painted white.

30. If you have three quarters, four dimes, and four pennies, you have $1.19. You also have the largest amount of money in coins without being able to make change for a dollar.

31. By raising your legs slowly and lying on your back, you can't sink in quicksand. (And you thought this list was useless).

32. The phrase "rule of thumb" is derived from an old English law, which stated that you couldn't beat your wife with anything wider that your thumb.

33. American Airlines saved $40,000 in '87 by eliminating one olive from each salad served in first class.

34. The first product Motorola started to develop was a record player for automobiles. At that time, the most known player on the market was the Victrola, so they called themselves Motorola.

35. Celery has negative calories! It takes more calories to eat a piece of celery than the celery has in it to begin with. It's the same with apples!

36. Chewing gum while peeling onions will keep you from crying!

37. The glue on Israeli postage stamps is certified kosher.

38. Guinness Book of Records holds the record for being the book most often stolen from Public Libraries.

39. Back in the mid to late 80's, an IBM compatible computer wasn't considered a hundred percent compatible unless it could run Microsoft's Flight Simulator game.

40. Astronauts are not allowed to eat beans before they go into space because passing wind in a space suit damages them.

WHAT DOES A KISS TASTE LIKE?

The day a teacher had a taste test with her students. She picked a little boy to do the first test. She blindfolded him, put a Hershey kiss in his mouth and asked, "Do you know what it is?"

"No, I don't," said the little boy.

"Okay, I'll give you a clue. It's the thing your daddy wants from your mom before he goes to work."

Suddenly, a little boy at the back of the room yelled, "Spit it out! It's a piece of ass!"

LITTLE LISA AND THE GOLDFISH

Little Lisa was in the garden filling up a hole in the dirt, when her neighbor peered over the fence. Interested in what the cheeky-faced youngster was up to, he politely asked, "What are you doing there, Lisa?"

"My goldfish died," replied Lisa tearfully without looking up, "and I've just buried him."

The neighbor was very concerned. "That's an awfully big hole for a goldfish, isn't it?"

Lisa patted down the last heap of dirt then replied, "That's because he's inside your damn cat."

NEVER LIE TO MOM

Brian Hester invited his mother over for dinner. During the course of the meal, Brian's mother couldn't help but keep noticing how beautiful Brian's roommate, Stephanie, was.

Mrs. Hester had long been suspicious of a relationship between Brian and his roommate, Stephanie, and this had only made her more curious.

Over the course of the evening, while watching the two react, Mrs. Hester started to wonder if there was more between Brian and his roommate, Stephanie, than met the eye.

Reading his Mon's thoughts, Brian volunteered, "I know what you must be thinking, but I assure you Stephanie and I are just roommates.

About a week later, Stephanie came to Brian saying, "Ever since your mother came to dinner, I've been unable to find the beautiful silver gravy ladle. You don't suppose she took it, do you?"

Brian said, "Well, I doubt it, but I'll send her an e-mail just to be sure."

"Dear Mother,
I'm not saying that you 'did' take the gravy ladle from the house, I'm not saying that you 'did not' take the gravy ladle. But the fact remains that one has been missing ever since you were here for dinner.
        Love Brian"

Several days later, Brian received a letter from his mother that read:

Dear Son,
I'm not saying that you 'do' sleep with Stephanie, and I'm not saying that you 'do not' sleep with Stephanie. But the fact remains that if she were sleeping in her own bed, she would have found the gravy ladle by now.

Love, Mom"

LEROY AND THE GATOR

A filthy rich man in North Carolina decided that he wanted to throw a party, so he invited Leroy, the only redneck in the neighborhood. He held the party around the pool in the backyard of his mansion.

Everyone was having a good time drinking, dancing, eating shrimp, oysters and BBQ and flirting with the women.

At the height of the party, the host said, "I have a 10 ft. man-eating gator in my pool and I'll give a million dollars to anyone who has the nerve to jump in."

The words were barely out of his mouth when there was a loud splash and everyone turned around and saw Leroy in the pool! Leroy was fighting the gator with all his might. Leroy was jabbing the gator in the eyes with his thumbs, throwing punches, head butts and choke holds, biting the gator on the tail and flipping the gator through the air like some kind of Judo Instructor.

Both Leroy and the gator were screaming and raising hell. Finally Leroy strangled the gator and let it float to the top like a K-Mart goldfish. Leroy then slowly climbed out of the pool.

Everyone was just staring at him in disbelief. Finally the host says, "Well, Leroy, I reckon I owe you a million dollars."

"I don't want it," said Leroy.

"You won the bet. How about half a million bucks then?"

"I don't want it," answered Leroy.

The host said, "Come on, I insist on giving you something, That was really amazing. How about a new Porsche, a Rolex and some stock options?"

266

"I don't want them." said Leroy.

Confused, the rich man asked, "Well, Leroy, then what do you want?"

Leroy said, "I want the name of the sumbitch who pushed me in the pool!"

EVERYONE HAS A PHOTOGRAPHIC MEMORY, SOME JUST DON'T HAVE FILM!

If you're not familiar with the work of Steven Wright, he's the famous scientist who once said: "I woke up one morning and all of my stuff had been stolen … and replaced by exact duplicates." His mind sees things differently than we do, to our amazement and amusement.

Here are more of his gems:

1. I'd kill for a Nobel Prize.
2. Borrow money from pessimists – they don't expect it back.
3. Half the people you know are below average.
4. 99% of lawyers give the rest a bad name.
5. 42.7% of all statistics are made up on the spot.
6. A conscience is what hurts when all your other parts feel so good.
7. A clear conscience is usually the sign of a bad memory.
8. If you want the rainbow, you gotta put up with the rain.
9. All those who believe in psycho-kinesis, raise my hand.
10. The early bird may get the worm, but the second mouse gets the cheese.
11. I almost had a psychic girlfriend, but she left me before we met.
12. OK, so what's the speed of dark?
13. How do you tell when you're out of invisible ink?
14. If everything seems to be going well, you have obviously overlooked something.
15. Depression is merely anger without enthusiasm.
16. When everything is coming your way, you're in the wrong lane.

17. Ambition is a poor excuse for not having enough sense to be lazy.

18. Hard work pays off in the future -- laziness pays off now.

19. I intend to live forever – so far, so good.

20. If Barbie is so popular, why do you have to buy her friends?

21. Eagles may soar, but weasels don't get sucked into jet engines.

22. What happened if you get scared half to death twice?

23. My mechanic told me, "I couldn't repair your brakes, so I made your horn louder."

24. Why do psychics have to ask you for your name?

25. If at first you don't succeed, destroy all evidence that you tried.

26. A conclusion is the place where you got tired of thinking.

27. Experience is something you don't get until just after you need it.

28. The hardness of the butter is proportional to the softness of the bread.

29. To steal ideas from one person is plagiarism; to steal from many is research.

30. The problem with the gene pool is that there is no lifeguard.

31. The sooner you fall behind, the more time you'll have to catch up.

32. The colder the x-ray table, the more your body is required to be on it.

33. Everyone has a photographic memory, some just don't have film!

QUOTE OF THE DAY

"Life isn't like a box of chocolates ... it's more like a jar of jalapeños. What you do today, might burn your ass tomorrow."

ANAL GLAUCOMA

A woman calls her boss one morning and tells him that she is staying home because she is not feeling well. "What's the matter?" he asks.

"I have a case of Anal Glaucoma," she says in a weak voice.

He asks, "What the hell is Anal Glaucoma?"

She responds: "I can't see my ass coming into work today."

FINALLY, THE BLONDE
JOKE TO END ALL BLONDE JOKES!

A blond woman was speeding down the road in her little red sports car and was pulled over by a woman police officer who was also a blonde. The blonde cop asked to see the blonde driver's license.

She dug through her purse and was getting progressively more agitated. "What does it look like?" she finally asked.

The policewoman replied, "It's square and it has your picture on it."

The driver finally found a square mirror, looked at it and handed it to the policewoman. "Here it is," she said.

The blonde officer looked at the mirror, then handed it back saying, "Okay, you can go. I didn't realize you were a cop."

BANKING

Send this to your bank and see what happens!

The letter below is an actual letter that was sent to a bank by a 96 year old woman. The bank manager thought it amusing enough to have it published in the New York Times.

Dear Sir:

I am writing to thank you for bouncing my check with which I endeavored to pay my plumber last month. By my calculations, three nanoseconds must have elapsed between his presenting the check and the arrival in my account of the funds needed to honor it. I refer, of course, to the automatic monthly deposits of my entire salary, an arrangement which, I admit, has been in place, for only eight years. You are to be commended for seizing that brief window of opportunity, and also for debiting my account $30 by way of penalty for the inconvenience caused your bank

My thankfulness springs from the manner in which this incident has caused me to rethink my errant financial ways. I noticed that whereas I personally attend to your telephone call and letters, when I try to contact you, I am confronted by the impersonal, overcharging, pre-recorded, faceless entity which your bank has become. From now on, I, like you, choose only to deal with a flesh-and-blood person.

My mortgage and loan repayments will therefore and hereafter no longer be automatic, but will arrive at your bank, by check, addressed personally and confidentially to an employee at your bank whom you must nominate. Be aware that it is an offense under the Postal Act for any other person to open such an envelope.

Please find attached an Application Contract Status which I require your chosen employee to complete. I am sorry it runs to eight pages, but in order that I know as much about him or her as your bank knows about me, there is no alternative. Please note that all copies of his or

273

her medical history must be countersigned by a Notary Public, and the mandatory details of his/her financial situation (income, debts, assets and liabilities) must be accompanied by documented proof. In due course, I will issue your employee with a PIN number which he/she must quote in dealings with me.

I regret that it cannot be shorter than 28 digits but, again, I have modeled it on the number of button presses required of me to access my account balance on your phone ban service. As they say, imitation is the sincerest form of flattery.

Let me level the playing field even further. When you call me, press buttons as follows: To make an appointment to see me, press 2. To query a missing payment, press 3. To transfer the call to my living room in case I am there presses 4. To transfer the call to my bedroom in case I am sleeping, press 5. To transfer the call to my toilet in case I am attending to nature, press 6. To transfer the call to my mobile phone if I am not at home, press 7. To leave a message on my computer, a password to access my computer is required. Password will be communicated to you at a later date to the Authorized Contact, press 8. To return to the main menu and to listen to options 1 through 7, press 9. To make a general complaint or inquiry, the contact will then be put on hold, pending the attention of my automated answering service. While this may, on occasion, involve a lengthy wait, uplifting music will play for the duration of the call.

Regrettably, but again following your example, I must also levy an establishment fee to cover the setting up of this new arrangement. May I wish you a happy, if ever so slightly less prosperous, New Year.

Your Humble Client

MOTHER-IN-LAW'S BURIAL

A man, his wife, and mother-in-law went on vacation to the Holy Land. While they were there, the mother-in-law passed away. The undertaker told them, "You can have her shipped home for $5,000, or you can bury her here in the Holy Land for $150.00."

The man thought about it and told him he would just have her shipped home.

The undertaker asked, "Why would you spend $5,000 to ship your mother-in-law home, when it would be wonderful to be buried here and spend only $150.00?"

The man said, "A man died here over 2000 years ago, he was buried and three days later, he rose from the dead. I can't take that risk.

DEAR DOGS AND CATS

The dishes with the paw print are yours and contain your food. The other dishes are mine and contain my food. Please note, placing a paw print in the middle of my plate and food does not stake a claim for it becoming your food and dish, nor do I find that aesthetically pleasing in the slightest.

The stairway was not designed by NASCAR and is not a racetrack. Beating me to the bottom is not the object. Tripping me doesn't help because I fall faster than you can run.

When I say to move, it means to go someplace else, not to switch positions with each other so there are still two of you in the way.

I cannot buy anything bigger than a king size bed. I am very sorry about this. Do not think I will continue sleeping on the couch to ensure your comfort. Dogs and cats can actually curl up in a ball when they sleep.

It is not necessary to sleep perpendicular to each other stretched out to the fullest extend possible. I also know that sticking tails straight out and having tongues hanging out the other end to maximize space is nothing but sarcasm.

For the last time, there is not a secret exit from the bathroom. If by some miracle I beat you there and manage to get the door shut, it is not necessary to claw, whine, meow, and try to turn the knob or get your paw under the edge and try to pull the door open. I must exit through the same door I entered. Also, I have been using the bathroom for years – canine or feline attendance is not mandatory.

The proper order is kiss me, then go smell the other dog or cat's butt. I cannot stress this enough!

To pacify you, my dear pets, I have posted the following message on our front door:

Rules for Non-Pet Owners who visit and like to complain about our pets.

1. They live here. You don't.

2. If you don't want their hair on your clothes, stay off the furniture. (That's why they call it "fur"nature.)

3. I like my pets a lot better than most people.

4. To you, it's an animal. To me, he/she is an adopted son/daughter who is short, hairy, walks on all fours and doesn't speak clearly.

Dogs and cats are better than kids. They eat less, don't ask for money all the time, are easier to train, usually come when called, never drive your car, don't hang out with drug-using friends, don't smoke or drink, don't worry about having to buy the latest fashions, don't wear your clothes, and don't need a gazillion dollars for college – and if they get pregnant, you can sell the children.

MA BELL STRIKES AGAIN

An elderly lady called her telephone company to report that her telephone failed to ring when her friends called – and that on the few occasions when it did ring, her pet dog always moaned right before the phone rang.

The telephone repairman proceeded to the scene, curious to see this psychic dog or senile elderly lady. He climbed a nearby telephone pole, hooked in his test set, and dialed the subscriber's house. The phone didn't ring right away, but the dog moaned loudly and the telephone began to ring. Climbing down from the pole, the telephone repairman found:

1. The dog was tied to the telephone system's ground wire via a steel chain and collar.
2. The wire connection to the ground rod was loose.
3. The dog was receiving 90 volts of signaling current when the phone number was called.
4. After a couple of such jolts, the dog would start moaning and then urinate on himself and the ground.
5. The wet ground would complete the circuit, thus causing the phone to ring.

Which demonstrates that some problems CAN be fixed by pissing and moaning.

BARBIE

Finally a Barbie I can relate to. At long last, here are some new Barbie Dolls to coincide with her and our aging gracefully. These are a bit more realistic ...

1. Bifocals Barbie. Comes with her own set of blended-lens fashioned frames in six wild colors (half-frames too!), neck chain, and large-print editions of Vogue and Martha Stewart Living.

2. Hot Flash Barbie. Press Barbie's bellybutton and watch her face turn beet red while tiny drops of perspiration appear on her forehead.

3. Facial Hair Barbie. As Barbie's hormone levels shift, see her whiskers grow. Available with teensy tweezers and magnifying mirror.

4. Flabby Arms Barbie. Hide Barbie's droopy triceps with these new, roomier-sleeved gowns. Good news on the tummy front, two-Muumuus with tummy-support panels are included.

5. Bunion Barbie. Years of disco dancing in stiletto heels have definitely taken their toll on Barbie's dainty arch feet. Soothe her sores with the pumice stone and plasters, then slip on soft terry mules.

6. No-More-Wrinkles Barbie. Erase those pesky crow's-feet and lip lines with a tube of Skin Sparkle-Spackle, from Barbie's own line of exclusive age-blasting cosmetics.

7. Soccer Mom Barbie. All that experience as a cheerleader is really paying off as Barbie dusts off her old high school megaphone to root for Babs and Ken, Jr. Comes with minivan in robin-egg blue or white and cooler filled with doughnuts holes and fruit punch.

8. Mid-life Crisis Barbie. It's time to ditch Ken. Barbie needs a change, and Alonzo (her personal trainer) is just what the doctor ordered, along with Prozac. They're hopping in her

new red Miata and heading for the Napa Valley to open a B&B. Includes a red tape of "Breaking Up Is Hard to Do."

9. Divorce Barbie. Sells for $199.00. Comes with Ken's house, Ken's car, and Ken's boat.

10. Recovery Barbie. Too many parties have finally caught up with the ultimate party girl. Now she does Twelve Steps instead of dance steps. Clean and sober, she's going to meetings religiously. Comes with a little copy of The Big Book and a six-pack of Diet Coke.

11. Post-Menopausal Barbie. This Barbie wets her pants when she sneezes, forgets where she puts things, and cries a lot. She is sick and tired of Ken sitting on the couch watching the tube, clicking through the channels. Comes with Depends and Kleenex. As a bonus this year, the book "Getting in Touch with Your Inner Self" is included.

LIVING WILL

The nation-wide interest in living wills in this country has exploded, following the sad case of Terri Schiavo. Here is one form of a Living Will that you can fill-in the blanks and print out for your own use.

Living Will: I, _____ (fill in the blank), being of sound mind and body, do not wish to be kept alive indefinitely by artificial means.

Under no circumstances should my fate be put in the hands of any peckerwood politicians who couldn't pass ninth-grade biology if their lives depended on it.

If a responsible amount of time passes and I fail to sit up and ask for a cold beer, it should be presumed that I won't ever get better.

When such a determination is reached, I hereby instruct my spouse, children and attending physicians to pull the plug, reel in the tubes, turn out the lights and call it a day.

Under no circumstances shall the members of the Legislature enact a special law to keep me on life-support machinery of any sort.

It is my wish that these boneheads mind their own doggone business, and pay attention instead to the health, education and future of the millions of Americans who aren't in the permanent coma, permanent vegetative state, or whatever you call it.

Under no circumstances shall any politicians butt into this case. I don't care how many fundamentalist votes there're trying to scrounge up for their run for the presidency in 2008, it is my wish that they play politics with someone else's life and leave me completely alone to die in peace.

I couldn't care less if a hundred religious zealots send e-mails to legislators in which they pretend to care about me. I don't know these people, and I certainly haven't authorized them to preach, pontificate or crusade on my behalf. They should mind their own business, too.

Most especially, under no circumstances shall I be allowed to live long enough for Jesse Jackson and his ever-present TV cameras to show-up at my bedside. If he is on his way, don't just pull the tubes, pull out a gun and shoot me, at least ten times to be sure.

If any of my family goes against my wishes and turns my case into a political cause, I hereby promise to come back from the grave and make his or her existence a living hell.

SELF A.A.A.D.D. TEST

Do you have A.A.A.D.D.? Recently, I was diagnosed with A.A.A.D.D. – Age Activated Attention Deficit Disorder. This is how it manifests:

I decided to wash my car.

As I start toward the garage, I notice that there is mail on the hall table. I decide to go through the mail before I wash the car.

I lay my car keys down on the table, put the junk mail in the trash can under the table, and notice that the trash can is full. So I decide to put the bills back on the table and take out the trash first.

But then I think, since I'm going to be near the mailbox when I take out the trash anyway, I may as well pay the bills first. I take my checkbook off the table, and see that there is only one check left.

My extra checks are in my desk in the study, so I go to my desk where I find the can of Coke that I had been drinking. I'm going to look for my checks, but first I need to push the Coke aside so that I don't accidentally knock it over.

I see that the Coke is getting warm, and I decide I should put it in the refrigerator to keep it cold. As I head toward the kitchen with the coke, a vase of flowers on the counter catches my eye ... they need water.

I set the Coke down on the counter, and I discover my reading glasses that I've been searching for all morning.

I decide I better put them back on my desk, but first I'm going to water the flowers. I set the glasses back down on the counter, fill a container with water and suddenly I spot the TV remote. Someone left it on the kitchen table.

I realize that tonight when we go to watch TV, I will be looking for the remote, but I won't remember that it's on the kitchen table, so I decide to put it back in the den where it belongs, but first I'll water the flowers.

I splash some water on the flowers, but most of it spills on the floor. So, I set the remote back down on the table, get some towels and wipe up the spill.

Then I head down the hall trying to remember what I was planning to do. At the end of the day: the car isn't washed, the bills aren't paid, there is a warm can of Coke sitting on the counter, the flowers aren't watered, there is still only one check in my checkbook, I can't find the remote, I can't find my glasses, and I don't remember what I did with the car keys.

Then when I try to figure out why nothing got done today, I'm really baffled because I know I was busy all day long, and I'm really tired.

I realize this is a serious problem, and I'll try to get some help for it, but first I'll check my e-mail.

Do me a favor, will you? Forward this message to everyone you know, because I don't remember to whom it has been sent.

Don't laugh ... if this isn't you yet, your day is coming!

SOME OF THE ARTIST OF THE 60'S ARE REVISITING THE HITS WITH NEW LYRICS TO ACCOMMODATE THE BABY BOOMERS:

1. Herman's Hermits – Mrs. Brown, you've got a lovely walker.
2. Bee Gees – How can you mend a broken hip?
3. Bobby Darin – Splish, splash, I was having a flash.
4. Ringo Starr – I get by with a little help from depends.
5. Roberta Flack – The first time ever I forgot your face.
6. Johnny Nash – I can't see clearly now.
7. Paul Simon – Fifty ways to love your liver.
8. Commodores – Once, twice, three times to the bathroom.
9. Marvin Gaye – Heard it through the Grape nuts.
10. Procol Harem – A whiter shade of hair.
11. Leo Sayer – You make me feel like napping.
12. The Temptations – Papa's got a Kidney Stone.
13. Abba – Denture Queen.
14. Tony Orlando – Knock 3 times on the ceiling if you hear me fall.
15. Helen Reddy – I am woman, hear me snore.
16. Willie Nelson – On the commode again.
17. Leslie Gore – It's my procedure and I'll cry if I want to.

CAKE OR BED

Husband is at home watching a football game when his wife interrupts "Honey, could you fix the light in the hallway? It's been flickering for weeks now."

He looks at her and says angrily, "Fix the light? Now? Does it look like I have a G.E. logo printed on my forehead? I don't think so."

"Well then, could you fix the fridge door? It won't close right." To which he replied, "Fix the fridge door? Does it look like I have Westinghouse written on my forehead? I don't think so."

"Fine," she says "then you could a least fix the steps to the front door. They are about to break." "I'm not a carpenter and I don't want to fix steps," he says, "does it look like I have Ace Hardware written on my forehead? I don't think so. I've had enough of you. I'm going to the bar!!!"

So he goes to the bar and drinks for a couple of hours. He starts to feel guilty about how he treated his wife and decides to go home and help out. As he enters the house he sees the hall light is working. As he goes to get a beer he notices the fridge door is fixed.

"Honey, how'd all this get fixed?"

She said "Well when you left I sat outside and cried. Just then a nice young man asked me what was wrong and I told him. He offered to do all the repairs and all I had to do was either go to bed with him or bake a cake."

He said "So what kind of cake did you bake him?"

She replied, "Helloooooo … do you see Betty Crocker written on my forehead? I don't think so."

PRINCESS AND THE FROG

This is a fairy tale that should have been read to all girls when they were little!

Once upon a time in a land far away, a beautiful, independent, self assured princess happened upon a frog as she sat contemplating ecological issues on the shores of an unpolluted pond in a verdant meadow near her castle.

The frog hopped into the princess' lap and said: "Elegant Lady, I was once a handsome prince, until an evil witch cast a spell upon me. One kiss from you, however, and I will turn back into the dapper, young prince that I am and then, my sweet, we can marry and set up housekeeping in your castle with my mother, where you can prepare my meals, clean my clothes, bear my children, and forever feel grateful and happy doing so.

That night, as the princess dined sumptuously on lightly sautéed frog legs seasoned in a white wine and onion cream sauce, she chuckled and thought to herself: I don't freakin think so!

YOU ONLY NEED TWO TOOLS

WC-40 and Duck tape.
If it doesn't move and should, use the WD-40.
If it shouldn't move and does, use the duct tape.

UNDERSTANDING ENGINEERS

What is the difference between Mechanical Engineers and Civil Engineers?
Mechanical Engineers build weapons. Civil Engineers build targets.

Normal people believe that if it isn't broken, don't fix it.
Engineers believe that if it isn't broken, it doesn't have enough features yet.

One day, an engineer was crossing a road when a frog called out to him and said, "If you kiss me, I'll turn into a beautiful princess."
He bent over, picked up the frog and put it in his pocket.
The frog spoke up again and said, "If you kiss me and turn me back into a beautiful princess, I will stay with you for one week."
The engineer took the frog out of his pocket, smiled at it and returned it to the pocket.
The frog then cried out, "If you kiss me and turn me back into a princess, I'll stay with you and do ANYTHING you want."
Again the engineer took the frog out, smiled at it and put it back into his pocket.
Finally, the frog asked, "What is the matter? I've told you I'm a beautiful princess, I'll stay with you for a week and do anything you want. Why won't you kiss me?"
The engineer said, "Look, I'm an engineer. A girlfriend for a week is nothing new, but a talking frog, now that's cool."

HOLY MOLY!

An Irish priest and a Rabbi found themselves sharing a compartment on a train.

After awhile, the priest opened a conversation by saying, "I know that, in your religion, you're not supposed to eat pork ... Have you actually ever tasted it?"

The Rabbi said, "I must tell the truth. Yes, I have, on the odd occasion."

Then the Rabbi had his turn of interrogation. He asked, "Your religion, too ... I know you're supposed to be celibate. But ..."

The priest replied, "Yes, I know what you're going to ask. I have succumbed once or twice."

There was silence for a while. Then the Rabbi peeped around the newspaper he was reading and said, "Better than pork, isn't it?"

WOMAN'S BEST FRIEND

A woman was leaving a convenience store with her morning coffee when she noticed a most unusual funeral procession approaching the nearby cemetery. A long black hearse was followed by a second long black hearse about 50 feet behind the first one. Behind the second hearse was a solitary woman walking a pit bull on a leash. Behind her, a short distance back, were about 200 women walking single file.

The woman couldn't stand her curiosity. She respectfully approached the woman walking the dog and said, "I'm so sorry for your loss, I know now is a bad time to disturb you, but I've never seen a funeral like this. Whose funeral is it?"

"My husband's."

"What happened to him?"

The woman replied, "My dog attacked and killed him."

She inquired further, "Well, who is in the second hearse?"

The woman answered, "My mother-in-law. She was trying to help my husband when the dog turned on her."

A poignant and thoughtful moment of silence passed between the two women.

"Can I borrow the dog?"

"Get in line."

291

HAVE YOU EVER WONDERED...

- Some people are like Slinkies. Not really good for anything, but you still can't help but smile when you see one tumble down the stairs.

- In the 60's, people took acid to make the world weird. Now the world is weird and people take Prozac to make it normal.

- How is it one careless match can start a forest fire, but it takes a whole box to start a campfire?

- Who was the first person to look at a cow and say, "I think I'll squeeze these dangly things here, and drink whatever comes out?"

- Who was the first person to say, "See that chicken there? I'm gonna eat the next thing that comes outta its butt."

TYPICAL GOLFER

A man and his wife walked into a dentist's office. The man said to the dentist, "Doc, I'm in one hell of a hurry! I have two buddies sitting out in my car waiting for us to play gold. So forget about the anesthetic and just pull the tooth and be done with it. We have a 10:00 AM tee time at the best golf course in town and it's 9:30 already. I don't have time to wait for the anesthetic to work!" The dentist thought to himself, "My goodness, this is surely a very brace man asking to have his tooth pulled without using anything to kill the pain." So the dentist ask him, "Which tooth is it sir?" The man turned to his wife and said, "Open your mouth, Honey, and show him."

PISSED ABOUT GAS

A young nun who worked for a local home health care agency and out making her rounds when she ran out of gas. As luck would have it, there was a gas station just one block away. She walked to the station to borrow a can with enough gas to start the car and drive to the station for a fill up. The attendant regretfully told her that the only gas can he owned had just been loaned out; but if she would care to wait, he was sure it would be back shortly.

Since the nun was on the way to see a patient, she decided not to wait and walked back to her car.

After looking through her car for something to carry to the station to fill with gas, she spotted a bedpan she was taking to the patient. Always resourceful, she carried it to the station, filled it with gasoline, and carried it back to her car.

As she was pouring the gas into the tank of her car, two men watched her from across the street. One of them turned to the other and said: "I know that it is said that Jesus turned water into wine, but if that car starts, I'm going to church every Sunday for the rest of my life."

WHY DID THE CHICKEN CROSS THE ROAD?

Dr Phil: The problem we have here is that this chicken won't realize that he must first deal with the problem on "THIS" side of the road before it goes after the problem on the "OTHER SIDE" of the road. What we need to do is help him realize how stupid he's acting by not taking on his "CURRENT" problems before adding "NEW" problems.

Oprah: Well I understand that the chicken is having problems, which is why he wants to cross this road so bad. So instead of having the chicken learn from his mistakes and take falls, which is a part of life, I'm going to give this chicken a car so that he can just drive across the road and not live his life like the rest of the chickens.

George W. Bush: We don't really care why the chicken crossed the road. We just want to know if the chicken is on our side of the road, or not. The chicken is either against us, or for us. There is no middle ground here.

Donald Rumsfeld: Now to the left of the screen, you can clearly see the satellite image of the chicken crossing the road.

Anderson Cooper/CNN: We have reason to believe there is a chicken, but we have not yet been allowed to have access to the other side of the road.

John Kerry: Although I voted to let the chicken cross the road, I am now against it! It was the wrong road to cross, and I was misled about the chicken's intentions. I am for it now, and will remain against it.

Judge Judy: That chicken crossed the road because he's GUILTY! You can see it in his eyes and the way he walks.

Pat Buchanan: To steal the job of a decent, hardworking American.

Martha Stewart: No one called me to warn me which way that chicken was going. I had a standing order at the Farmer's Market to sell my eggs when the price dropped to a certain level. No little bird gave me any insider information.

Dr. Seuss: Did the chicken cross the road? Did he cross it with a toad? Yes, the chicken crossed the road, but why it crossed I've not been told.

Ernest Hemingway: To die in the rail. Alone.

Jerry Falwell: Because the chicken was gay! Can't you people see the plain truth in front of your face? The chicken was going to the "other side." That's why they call it the other side. Yes, my friends, that chicken is gay. And if you eat that chicken, you will become gay too. I say we boycott all chickens until we sort out this abomination that the liberal media whitewashes with seemingly harmless phrases like "the other side." That chicken should not be free to cross the road. It's as plain and simple as that!"

Grandpa: In my day we didn't ask why the chicken crossed the road. Somebody told us the chicken crossed the road, and that was good enough.

Barbara Waters: Isn't that interesting? In a few moments, we will be listening to the chicken tell for the first time, the heart warming story of how it experienced a serious case of molting, and went on to accomplish its life long dream of crossing the road.

John Lennon: Imagine all the chickens in the world crossing roads together – in peace.

Aristotle: It is the nature of chickens to cross the road.

Bill Gates: I have just released eChicken 2005, which will not only cross roads, but will lay eggs, file your important documents, and balance your check book. Internet explorer is an integral part of eChicken. The Platform is much more stable and will never cra...#@&&^(%/... reboot.

Albert Einstein: Did the chicken really cross the road, or did her road move beneath the chicken?

Bill Clinton: I did not cross the road with THAT chicken. What is your definition of chicken?

Al Gore: I invented the chicken!

Colonel Sanders: Did I miss one?

A REAL MAN

A real man is a woman's best friend. He will never stand her up and never let her down. He will reassure her when she feels insecure and comfort her after a bad day.

He will inspire her to do things she never thought she could do; to live without fear and forget regret. He will enable her to express her deepest emotions and give in to her most intimate desires. He will make sure she always feels as though she's the most beautiful woman in the room and will enable her to be the most confident, sexy, seductive, and invincible.

No wait...sorry...I'm thinking of wine. It's wine that does all that....sorry. Never mind.

LETTER TO THE ANIMALS IN YOUR HOUSE

The dishes with the paw print are yours and contain your food. The other dishes are mine and contain my food. Please note, placing a paw print in the middle of my plate and food does not stake a claim for it becoming your food and dish, nor do I find that aesthetically pleasing in the slightest.

The stairway was not designed by NASCAR and is not a racetrack. Beating me to the bottom is not the object. Tripping me doesn't help because I fall faster than you can run.

I cannot buy anything bigger than a king-size bed. I am very sorry about this. Do not think I will continue sleeping on the couch to ensure your comfort. Dogs and cats can actually curl up in a ball when they sleep. It is not necessary to sleep perpendicular to each other stretched out to the fullest extent possible. I also know that sticking tails straight out and having tongues hanging out the other end to maximize space is nothing by sarcasm.

For the last time, there is not a secret exit from the bathroom. If by some miracle I beat you there and manage to get the door shut, it is not necessary to claw, whine, meow, try to turn the knob, or get your paw under the edge and try to pull the door open. I must exit through the same door I entered. I have been using the bathroom for years …canine or feline attendance is not mandatory.

The proper order is kiss me, then go smell the other dog or cat's butt. I cannot stress this enough!

To pacify you, my dear pets, I have posted the following message on our front door:

Rules for Non-Pet Owners Who Visit and Like to Complain About Out Pets:
1. They live here. You don't.

2. If you don't want hair on your clothes, stay off the furniture. (That's why they call it "fur"nature).
3. I like my pets a lot better than I like most people.
4. To you, it's an animal. To me, he/she is an adopted son/daughter who is short, hairy, walks on all fours, and does not speak clearly.

Remember: Dogs and cats are better than kids because they; eat less, don't ask for money all the time, are easier to train, usually come when called, never drive your car, don't hang out with drug-using friends, don't smoke or drink, don't worry about having to buy the latest fashions, don't wear your clothes, don't need a gazillion dollars for college, and if they get pregnant, you can sell their children.

COUNTRY BY CHOICE

Will we still be the Country of choice and still be America if we continue to make the changes forced on us by the people from other countries that came to live in America because it is the Country of Choice ???

All we have to say is, when will they do something about MY RIGHTS?

I celebrate Christmas....but because it isn't celebrated by everyone....we can no longer say Merry Christmas. Now it has to be Season's Greetings.

It's not Christmas vacation, it's Winter Break. Isn't it amazing how this winter break ALWAYS occurs over the Christmas Holiday?

We've gone so far the other way, bent over backwards to not offend anyone, that I am now being offended. But it seems that no one has a problem with that.

DEGREES OF BLONDES

First Degree: A married couple were asleep when the phone rang at 2 in the morning. The wife (undoubtedly blonde) picked up the phone, listened a moment and said, "How should I know, that's 200 miles from here!" and hung up. The husband said, "Who was that?" The wife said, "I don't know, some woman wanting to know if the coast is clear."

Second Degree: Two blondes are walking down the street. One notices a compact on the sidewalk and leans down to pick it up. She opens it, looks in the mirror and says, "Humm, this person looks familiar." The second blonde says, "Here, let me see!" So the first blonde hands her the compact. The second one looks in the mirror and says, "You dummy, it's me!"

Third Degree: A blonde suspects her boyfriend of cheating on her, so she goes out and buys a gun. She goes to his apartment unexpectedly and when she opens the door she finds him in the arms of a redhead. Well, the blonde is really angry. She opens her purse to take out the gun, and as she does so, she is overcome with grief. She takes the gun and puts it to her head. The boyfriend yells, "No, honey, don't do it!!!" The blonde replies, "Shut up, you're next!"

Fourth Degree: A blonde was bragging about her knowledge of state capitals. She proudly says, "Go ahead, ask me, I know all of them." A friend says, "OK, what's the capital of Wisconsin?" The blonde replies, "Oh, that's easy: W."

Fifth Degree: What did the blonde ask her doctor when he told her she was pregnant?
"Is it mine?"

Sixth Degree: Bambi, a blonde in her fourth year as a UCLA freshman, sat in her US Government class. The professor asked Bambi if she knew what Roe vs Wade was about. Bambi pondered the

302

question then finally said, "That was the decision George Washington had to make before he crossed the Delaware."

Seventh Degree: Returning home from work, a blonde was shocked to find her house ransacked and burglarized. She telephoned the police at once and reported the crime. The police dispatcher broadcast the call on the radio, and a K-9 Unit, patrolling nearby was the first to respond. As the K-9 officer approached the house with his dog on a leash, the blonde ran out on the porch, shuddered at the sight of the cop and his dog, then sat down on the steps. Putting her face in her hands, she moaned, "I come home to find all my possessions stolen. I call the police for help, and what do they do? They send me a BLIND policeman."

MAKE YOU SMILE

You can't read this and stay in a bad mood!

1. How do you catch a unique rabbit? Unique up on it!
2. How do you catch a tame rabbit? Tame way, unique up on it!
3. How do crazy people go through the forest? They take the psycho path.
4. How do you get Holy Water? You boil the hell out of it.
5. What do fish say when they hit a concrete wall? Dam!
6. What do Eskimos get from sitting on the ice too long? Polaroid's.
7. What do you call a boomerang that doesn't work? A stick.
8. What do you call cheese that isn't yours? Nacho Cheese.
9. What do you call Santa's Helpers? Subordinate Clauses.
10. What do you call four bullfighters in quicksand? Quattro Sinko.
11. What do you get from a pampered cow? Spoiled milk.
12. What do you get when you cross a snowman with a vampire? Frostbite.
13. What lies at the bottom of the ocean and twitches? A nervous wreck.
14. What's the difference between roast beef and pea soup? Anyone can roast beef
15. Where do you find a dog with no legs? Right were you left him.
16. Why do gorillas have big nostrils? Because they have big fingers.
17. Why don't blind people like to sky dive? Because it scares the dog.
18. What kind of coffee was served on the Titanic? Sanka.

19. What is the difference between a Harley and a Hoover? The location of the dirt bag.

20. Why did Pilgrims' pants always fall down? Because they wore their belt buckle on their hat.

21. What's the difference between a bad golfer and a bad skydiver? Bad golfer goes, whack, Dang! A bad skydiver goes, Dang, whack.

22. How are a Texas Tornado and a Tennessee divorce the same? Somebody's gonna lose a trailer.

Now admit it. At least one of these made you smile.

THE CHRISTMAS CLOSING

'Twas an hour before closing, and the agents were tense,
To close Christmas Eve just didn't make sense.
But the seller was booked on the 6 o'clock flight
And had warned, "There will be a Closing Tonight!"

The agents agreed because business was dead,
And visions of commission checks danced in their heads.
The loan was approved by the lender's good grace,
Everyone knew 'twas a borderline case.

The buyers divorced, remarried again,
Divorced once more, and now were just friends.
The loan package completed to the closer was carried,
With instructions to close before they remarried.

The title policy arrived via UPS,
From page one through sixteen, a terrible MESS!
An improper legal, 3 judgments, a lien,
But a few lines on page seven, looked pretty clean.

The title was cleared and the closing was set,
But to finish today was not a sure bet.
The closer dashed in waving her HUD,
It was covered with whiteout, coffee and crud.

But down in the corner you barely could see,
That the buyer still owed a buck thirty-three.
So the closer extracted a bill from her compact,
And the agents agreed to the rest on the contract.

To add some interest, the seller revealed,
To everyone's horror – the well wasn't sealed.
And, oh yes, he wanted to change the disclosure,
His mother just died of RADON EXPOSURE.

Everything else in his house was OK
(His cracked floors and walls were always that way).
About that time the buyer chimed in,
"We'd like to continue, but before we begin,

I noticed these papers – I'm likely to blame,
But I gave my agents the wrong legal name,
And one more thing I had hoped to avoid,
Does it really matter if I'm self-employed?"

About this time the close exploded.
She pulled out a gun and said it was loaded.
Everyone froze and sat there amazed,
She frothed at the mouth and her eyes were both glazed.

More rapid that eagles, her curses they came;
She bristled and spouted and called them BAD names.
"THE CLOSING IS OFF, DO I MAKE MYSELF CLEAR?
MERRY CHRISTMAS TO ALL - NOW GET OUT OF HERE!"

ANGELS WITH ATTITUDES

- Grant me the serenity to accept the things I cannot change, the courage to change the things I cannot accept, the wisdom to hide the bodies of those people I had to kill today because they pissed me off.

- And also, help me to be careful of the toes I step on today as they may be connected to the ass that I may have to kiss tomorrow.

- Help me to always give 100% at work....

- 12% on Monday

- 23% on Tuesday

- 40% on Wednesday

- 20% on Thursday

- 5% on Fridays

- And help me to remember....when I'm having a really bad day, and it seems that people are trying to piss me off, that it takes 42 muscles to frown and only 4 to extend my middle finger and tell them to bite me!

MOUSE BALLS

This apparently was a real memo sent out by a computer company to its employees in all seriousness, but it also went out to all field engineers about a computer peripheral problem.

If a mouse fails to operate or should it perform erratically, it may need a ball replacement. Mouse balls are now available as FRU (Field Replacement Units). Because of the delicate nature of this procedure, replacement of mouse balls should only be attempted by properly trained personnel.

Before proceeding, determine the type of mouse ball by examining the underside of the mouse. Domestic balls will be larger and harder than foreign balls. Ball removal procedures differ depending upon the manufacturer of the mouse. Foreign balls can be replaced using the pop off method. Domestic balls are replaced by using the twist off method.

Mouse balls are not usually static sensitive. However, excessive handling can result in sudden discharge. Upon completion of ball replacement, the mouse may be used immediately.

It is recommended that each person have a pair of spare balls for maintaining optimum customer satisfaction. Any customer missing his balls should contact the local personnel in charge of removing and replacing these necessary items.

Please keep in mind that a customer without properly working balls is an unhappy customer.

THAT'S WHAT FRIENDS ARE FOR

1. When you are sad - I will help you get drunk and plot revenge against the sorry bastard who made you sad.

2. When you are blue - I will try to dislodge whatever is choking you.

3. When you are scared - I will rag on you about it every chance I get.

4. When you are worried - I will tell you horrible stories about how much worse it could be and to quit whining.

5. When you are confused - I will use little words.

6. When you are sick - Stay the hell away from me until you are well again. I don't want whatever you have.

7. When you fall - I will point and laugh at your clumsy ass.

This is my oath...I pledge it till the end. "Why?" you ask, because you are my friend.

Remember: A good friend will help you move. A really good friend will help you move a body. Let me know if I ever need to bring a shovel.

THINKING OUTSIDE THE BOX

You are driving down the road in your car on a wild, stormy night, when you pass a bus stop and you see three people waiting for the bus:

1. An old lady who looks as if she is about to die.
2. An old friend who once saved your life.
3. The perfect partner you have been dreaming about.

Which one would you choose to offer a ride to, knowing that there could only be one passenger in your car?

Think before you continue reading.

You could pick up the old lady, because she is going to die, and thus you should save her first.

Or you could take the old friend because he once saved your life, and this would be the perfect chance to pay him back.

However, you may never be able to find your perfect mate again.

The candidate who was hired (out of 200 applicants) had no trouble coming up with his answer. He simply answered; "I would give the car keys to my old friend, and let him take the lady to the hospital. I would stay behind and wait for the bus with the partner of my dreams."

Sometimes, we gain more if we are able to give up our stubborn thought limitations. Never forget to "Think Outside the Box."

HOWEVER...,the correct answer is to run the old lady over and put her out of her misery, have sex with the perfect partner on the hood of the car, then drive off with the old friend for a few beers. God, I just love happy endings.

BUTTER

Margarine was originally manufactured to fatten turkeys. When it killed the turkeys, the people who had put all the money into the research wanted a payback, so they put their heads together to figure out what to do with this product to get their money back. It was a white substance with no food appeal so they added the yellow coloring and sold it to people to use in place of butter. How do you like it? They have come out with some clever new flavorings.

DO YOU KNOW...the difference between margarine and butter?

- Both have the same amount of calories.

- Butter is slightly higher in saturated fats at 8 grams compared to 5 grams.

- Eating margarine can increase heart disease in women by 53% over eating the same amount of butter, according to a recent Harvard Medical Study.

- Eating butter increases the absorption of many other nutrients in other foods.

- Butter tastes much better than margarine and it can enhance the flavors of other foods.

- Butter has many nutritional benefits where margarine has a few only because they are added!

- Butter has been around for centuries where margarine has been around for less than 100 years.

And now, for Margarine...

- Very high in trans fatty acids.

- Triple risk of coronary heart disease.

- Increases total cholesterol and LCL (this is the bad cholesterol) and lowers HDL cholesterol, (the good cholesterol).

- Increases the risk of cancers up to five fold.

- Lowers quality of breast milk.

- Decreases immune response.

- Decreases insulin response.

- And here's the most disturbing fact...Margarine is but ONE MOLECULE away from being PLASTIC.

These facts alone was enough to have me avoiding margarine for life and anything else that is hydrogenated (this means hydrogen is added, changing the molecular structure of the substance).

Try this yourself: Purchase a tub of margarine and leave it in your garage or shaded area. Within a couple days you will note a couple things:

- No flies, not even those pesky fruit flies will go near it (that should tell you something).

- It does not rot or smell differently because it has no nutritional value; nothing will grow on it. Even those teeny weeny microorganisms will not find a home to grow. Why? Because it is nearly plastic. Would you melt your Tupperware and spread that on your toast?

ELMO

There is a factory in America which makes Tickle Me Elmo toys. The toy laughs when you tickle it under the arm. A new employee is hired at the Tickle Me Elmo factory and she reports for her first day promptly a 0800. The next day at 0845 there is a knock at the Personnel Manager's door. The Foreman from the assembly line throws open the door and begins to rant about the new employee. He complains that she is incredibly slow and the whole line is backing up, putting the entire production line behind schedule.

The Personnel Manager decides he needs to see this for himself, so the two men march down to the factory floor. When they get there the line is so backed up that there are Tickle Me Elmo's all over the factory floor and they are really beginning to pile up.

At the end of the line stands the new employee surrounded by mountains of Tickle Me Elmo's. She has a roll of plush red fabric and a huge bag of small marbles. The two men watched in amazement as she cuts a little piece of fabric, wraps it around two marbles and begins to carefully sew the little package between Elmo's legs.

The Personnel Manager bursts into laughter. After several minutes of hysterics, he pulls himself together and approaches the woman. "I'm sorry," he says to her, barely able to keep a straight face, "but I think you misunderstood the instructions I gave you yesterday."

"Your job is to give Elmo test tickles."

SNAPDRAGONS

I just wanted you to know I have entered the snapdragon part of my life.

Part of me has snapped...And the rest of me is draggin.

THE LAWYER

A very successful lawyer parked his brand new Lexus in front of the office, ready to show it off to his colleagues. As he got out, a truck came along too close to the curb and completely tore off the driver's door.

Fortunately, a cop in a police car was close enough to see the accident and pulled up behind the Lexus, his lights flashing. But, before the cop had a chance to ask any questions, the lawyer started screaming hysterically about how his Lexus, which he had just picked up the day before, was now completely ruined and would never be the same, no matter how the body shop tried to make it new again.

After the lawyer finally wound down from his rant, the cop shook his head in disgust and disbelief. "I can't believe how materialistic you lawyers are," he said. "You are so focused on your possessions that you neglect the most important things in life."

"How can you say such a thing?" asked the lawyer.

The cop replied, "Don't you even realize that your left arm is missing? It got ripped off when the truck hit you!"

"Oh, my God!" screamed the lawyer. "My Rolex!"

COMMENTS MADE IN THE YEAR 1955

- I'll tell you one thing, if things keep going the way they are, it's going to be impossible to buy a week's groceries for $20.

- Have you seen the new cars coming out next year? It won't be long before $2000 will only buy a used car.

- If cigarettes keep going up in price, I'm going to quit. A quarter a pack is ridiculous.

- Did you hear the post office is thinking about charging a dime just to mail a letter?

- If they raise the minimum wage to $1, nobody will be able to hire outside help at the store.

- When I first started driving, who would have thought gas would someday cost 29 cents a gallon. Guess we'd be better off leaving the car in the garage.

- Kids today are impossible. Those duck tail hair cuts make it impossible to stay groomed. Next thing you know, boys will be wearing their hair as long as the girls.

- I'm afraid to send my kids to the movies any more. Ever since they let Clark Gable get by with saying "damn" in Gone With The Wind. It seems every new movie has either "hell" or "damn" in it.

- I read the other day where some scientist thinks it's possible to put a man on the moon by the end of the century. They even have some fellows they call astronauts preparing for it down in Texas.

- Did you see where some baseball player just signed a contract for $75,000 a year just to play ball? It wouldn't surprise me if someday they'll be making more than the President.

- I never thought I'd see the day all our kitchen appliances would be electric. They are even making electric typewriters now.

- It's too bad things are so tough nowadays. I see where a few married women are having to work to make ends meet.

- It won't be long before young couples are going to have to hire someone to watch their kids so they can both work.

- Marriage doesn't mean a thing any more; those Hollywood stars seem to be getting divorced at the drop of a hat.

- I'm just afraid the Volkswagen car is going to open the door to a whole lot of foreign business.

- Thank goodness, I won't live to see the day when the Government takes half our income in taxes. I sometimes wonder if we are electing the best people to congress.

- The drive-in-restaurant is convenient in nice weather, but I seriously doubt they will ever catch on.

- There is no sense going to Lincoln or Omaha anymore for a weekend. It costs nearly $15 a night to stay in a hotel.

- No one can afford to be sick any more; $35 a day in the hospital is too rich for my blood.

- If they think I'll pay 50 cents for a hair cut, forget it.

NUDE BEACH

A mother and father take their 6-year old son to a nude beach in Tampa. As the boy walks along the sand, he notices that many of the women have boobs bigger than his mother's, so he goes back to ask her why. He tells her son, "The bigger they are, the sillier the lady is."

The boy, pleased with the answer, goes to play in the ocean but returns to till his mother that many of the men have larger things than his dad does. She replies, "The bigger they are, the dumber the man is."

Again satisfied with the answer, the boy goes back to the ocean to play. Shortly thereafter, the boy returns again, and promptly tells his mother: "Daddy is talking to the silliest lady on the beach, and the longer he talks, the dumber he gets."

COMPUTER TECH SUPPORT VS IDIOT SUPPORT

Tech Support: What kind of computer do you have?
Customer: A white one.

Customer: Hi, this is Celine. I can't get my diskette out.
TS: Have you tried pushing the eject Button?
Customer: Yes, sure, it's really stuck.
TS: That doesn't sound good; I'll make a note.
Customer: No, wait a minute....I haven't inserted it yet....it's still on my desk...Sorry!

TS: Click on the "my computer" icon on the left of the screen.
Customer: You're left or my left?

TS: Good day. How may I help you?
Customer: Hello...I can't print.
TS: Would you click on "start" for me and ...
Customer: Listen pay; don't start getting technical on me. I'm not Bill Gates.

Customer: Hi, good afternoon, this is Martha, I can't print. Every time I try, it says "Can't find printer". I've even lifted the printer and placed it in front of the monitor, but the computer still says he can't find it ...

Customer: I have problems printing in red...
TS: Do you have a color printer?
Customer: Aaaah.........thank you.

TS: What's on your monitor now, ma'am?
Customer: A teddy bear my boyfriend bought for me at the 7-11.

Customer: My keyboard is not working anymore.
TS: Are you sure it's plugged into the computer?

Customer:	No, I can't get behind the computer.
TS:	Pick up your keyboard and walk 10 paces back.
Customer:	OK.
TS:	Did the keyboard come with you?
Customer:	Yes.
TS:	That means the keyboard is not plugged in. Is there another keyboard?
Customer:	Yes, there's another one here. Ah...that one does work...

| TS: | Your password is the small letter "a" as in apple, a capital letter V as in Victor, the number 7. |
| Customer: | Is that 7 in capital letters? |

Customer:	Can't get on the Internet.
TS:	Are you sure you used the right password?
Customer:	Yes, I'm sure. I saw my colleague do it.
TS:	Can you tell me what the password was?
Customer:	Five stars

TS:	What anti-virus program do you use?
Customer:	Netscape.
TS:	That's not an anti-virus program.
Customer:	Oh, sorry...Internet explorer.

| Customer: | I have a huge problem. A friend has placed a screen saver on my computer, but every time I move the mouse, it disappears. |

TS:	How may I help you?
Customer:	I'm writing my first email.
TS:	OK, and what seems to be the problem?
Customer:	Well, I have the letter ""a" in the address, but how do I get the circle around it?

A woman customer called the Canon help desk with a problem with her printer.

| TS: | Are you running it under windows? |

Customer:	No, my desk is next to the door, but that is a good point. The man sitting in the cubical next to me is under a window, and his printer is working fine.
TS:	"Okay, Bob, let's press the control and escape keys at the same time. That brings up a task list in the middle of the screen. Now type the letter "P" to bring up the Program Manager."
Customer:	I don't have a P.
TS:	On your keyboard, Bob.
Customer:	What do you mean?
TS:	"P"...on your keyboard, Bob.
Customer:	I'm not going to do that!

Compiler's Bio

Robert D. Kramer is a graduate of Ohio University and served in the US Air Force during the Vietnam era. He has worked in the corporate America banking for forty-two years. Robert is also Director Emeritus for the Salvador Dali Museum in St. Petersburg, Florida and past Director of the Mahaffee Theater, also located in St. Petersburg, FL.

www.ingramcontent.com/pod-product-compliance
Lightning Source LLC
Chambersburg PA
CBHW060835280326
41934CB00007B/797